MENLO SCHOOL

·MENLO COLLEGE·

founded 1915

Gift of

College Student Council

Library Fund

Established Fall of 1972

THE TASTE OF OUR TIME

Collection planned and directed by

ALBERT SKIRA

BIOGRAPHICAL AND CRITICAL STUDY

BY

LIONELLO VENTURI

Translated from the Italian by James Emmons

ROUAULT

Title page:
Figures on the Steps, Park of Versailles, 1910.
Watercolor. Musée d'Art Moderne, Paris.

*

Distributed by Crown Publishers, Inc.
419 Park Avenue South, New York, N.Y. 10016

© 1959 by Editions d'Art Albert Skira, Geneva
Library of Congress Catalog Card Number: 59-7253
New edition 1972

CHRONOLOGICAL SURVEY

1871 Birth of Georges Rouault on May 27th in the cellar of a house in the Belleville district of Paris (51, rue de la Villette) during the bombardment of the city by government troops in the troubled days of the Commune. His father Alexandre Rouault, a native of Brittany, was a cabinetmaker employed at the Pleyel piano factory; his mother, née Marie-Louise Champdavoine, was Parisian.

1881 Often stays with his maternal grandfather Alexandre Champdavoine, who has a taste for art and is a great admirer of Daumier, Courbet and Manet; he collects prints of their works which he shows to his young grandson.

1885- Apprenticed to a stained-glass maker named Tamoni; his
1890 second employer is Georges Hirsch, a restorer of old stained glass. Attends evening classes at the Ecole des Arts Décoratifs. Out of loyalty to Hirsch he turns down a chance to collaborate with the painter Albert Besnard on a set of stained-glass windows designed by the latter for the Ecole de Pharmacie. Decides to devote himself to painting.

1891 Enters Elie Delaunay's studio at the Ecole des Beaux-Arts.

1892 When Delaunay dies, his studio is taken over by Gustave Moreau, who thus becomes the teacher of Rouault, Matisse, Marquet, Lehmann, Bussy, Evenepoel, Manguin, Piot and Camoin. With a series of religious subjects Rouault wins first prize in his class.

1893 Now Gustave Moreau's favorite pupil, he competes for the Prix de Rome with "Samson at the Mill" but is unsuccessful.

1893 Opening of the Vollard Gallery in Paris.

1894 Rouault is awarded the Prix Chenavard for "The Child Jesus among the Doctors."

1895 Wins the Prix Fortin d'Ivry and competes for the Prix de Rome with "Christ mourned by the Holy Women" but is again unsuccessful. Acting on Moreau's advice he leaves the Ecole des Beaux-Arts. Exhibits at the Salon des Artistes Français and receives an award. Paints a series of sacred and profane scenes set in fantastic landscapes.

1895 Cézanne exhibition at Vollard's.

1898 Death of Gustave Moreau. In him Rouault loses a friend and mentor whose memory he was to venerate all his life. Becomes curator of the Gustave Moreau Museum.
His family leaves for Algeria; remaining behind in Paris, Rouault goes through a period of pecuniary difficulties and spiritual unrest.

1898 Matisse exhibits "La Desserte."

1899 Toulouse-Lautrec does a set of pastel drawings, "The Circus." Nabi Exhibition entitled "Homage to Odilon Redon" at Durand-Ruel's. Paul Signac publishes "D'Eugène Delacroix au Néo-Impressionnisme."

1900 Awarded a bronze medal at the Centennial Exhibition of French Art held in connection with the Paris World's Fair.

1901 Visits the Abbey of Ligugé in Poitou where he meets the novelist J. K. Huysmans.

1901 Death of Toulouse-Lautrec. Van Gogh exhibition at Bernheim-Jeune's. First Picasso exhibition at Vollard's; beginning of his Blue Period.

1902 After an illness Rouault convalesces at Evian, on the Lake of Geneva.
Begins exhibiting at the Salon des Indépendants.

1903 Takes part in founding the Salon d'Automne, with Desvallières, Matisse, Marquet, Piot and the critic Rambosson, and shows two pictures at the first exhibition.

1903 Death of Gauguin. Vollard publishes "The Imitation of Christ" illustrated with 216 woodcuts by Maurice Denis.

1904 March. Rouault meets the Catholic writer Léon Bloy; they become close friends and Bloy's influence is very strong for a time.
Exhibits at the Salon d'Automne: eight oil paintings (prostitutes, clowns, acrobats, Pierrot) and 32 watercolors and pastels, all in his new manner. The public jeers at these "dark" pictures but the critics see great promise in them.
Paints landscapes and many pictures of odalisques, clowns, circus scenes, and prostitutes.

1904 Large Cézanne exhibition at the Salon d'Automne. Matisse's first one-man show at Vollard's.

1905 Exhibits three important works at the Salon d'Automne—not, however, in the Fauve room. One is a triptych entitled "Prostitutes," one of the side panels of which represents Monsieur and Madame Poulot, two characters in Léon Bloy's novel "La Femme pauvre."

1905 Cézanne finishes "Les Grandes Baigneuses."
Derain and Matisse work together at Collioure; Matisse paints "Luxe, calme et volupté."
Meeting of Picasso and Apollinaire.

1906- Rouault paints ceramics and glazed earthenware, fired by
1907 Methey, who introduces him to Ambroise Vollard and Odilon Redon. Visit to Bruges.

1906 Matisse exhibits "The Joy of Life" at the Salon des Indépendants.
Death of Cézanne.
Gauguin exhibition at the Salon d'Automne.
Vollard buys up all the pictures in Vlaminck's studio.

1907 Picasso finishes "Les Demoiselles d'Avignon" and meets Braque.
Marquet's first one-man show at Druet's.

1908 Rouault marries Marthe Le Sidaner, sister of the painter Henry Le Sidaner. Four children were born to them: Geneviève, Isabelle, Michel and Agnès.
Begins his series of "Judges" and "Tribunals" inspired by trials at the Tribunal de la Seine, which he attended for nearly a year at the suggestion of his friend Granier, deputy public prosecutor. He also paints poor people, peasants and workers.

1908 Braque exhibits at Kahnweiler's; in "Gil Blas" the critic Louis Vauxcelles accuses him of reducing everything to "little cubes."

1909 A group of Belgian painters (Van den Berghe, Servaes, Permeke, Gustave and Léon de Smet) work together in the village of Laethem-Saint-Martin.

1910 February 25-March 5. Rouault's first one-man show at the Druet Gallery.

1910 Death of the Douanier Rousseau.

1911 Lives at Versailles. Close friendship with Jacques and Raïssa Maritain. Takes up social themes: peasants, workers, family life, portraits.

1911 Cubist rooms at the Indépendants and the Salon d'Automne.

1913 Attracted at first by his work as a ceramist, Vollard now buys up all the pictures in Rouault's studio.
Returns to religious subjects.

1913 Utrillo's first one-man show at Eugène Blot's.
Apollinaire publishes "Les Peintres cubistes."
1914 Derain paints "The Last Supper."
1916 Death of Odilon Redon.

1917 Vollard is now his sole agent; he later fits out a studio on the top floor of his own home to enable Rouault to complete several hundred unfinished works.
From 1917 to 1927 Rouault concentrates on the illustration of books, the most monumental of which is "Miserere."

1918 He abandons watercolors and gouache and reverts to oil painting. Sacred subjects, bearing mostly on the Passion of Christ. Uses a brighter palette. Almost ceases to exhibit.

1918 Death of Guillaume Apollinaire.

1919 Bought by the State in 1917, his "Child Jesus among the Doctors" is installed in the Musée d'Unterlinden, Colmar. This was the first of Rouault's paintings to enter a museum.

1919 Maurice Denis and Georges Desvallières found the "Studios of Sacred Art."

1920 Rouault exhibition at the Galerie La Licorne.

1920 Death of Modigliani. Picasso paints in a neo-classical style. Matisse paints a series of odalisques.

1921 Michel Puy publishes the first monograph on Rouault.

1922 One-man show at the Barbazanges Gallery.

1924 April 22-May 2. Large Rouault retrospective at Druet's. Awarded the Legion of Honor. Publishes poems, articles and letters in various reviews.

1925 Gromaire paints and exhibits "War" at the Indépendants.

1926 Rouault publishes his "Souvenirs Intimes," illustrated with lithographs. Georges Charensol publishes his book on Rouault (40 plates).

1929 Sets and costumes for a ballet by Diaghilev: "The Prodigal Son," with music by Prokofiev.

1930 The purchasing committee of the Musée du Luxembourg recommends the acquisition of a painting by Rouault, but the Ministry of Fine Arts vetoes the proposal. Holiday in the Valais (Switzerland). Begins work on color etchings for ''Le Cirque de l'Etoile Filante,'' for which he writes the text himself, and for ''Passion'' and ''Le Cirque'' written by André Suarès (the latter is still unpublished).
First Rouault exhibitions outside France: London (St. George's Gallery), Munich (Neumann Gallery), New York (Brummer Gallery) and Chicago (Arts Club).

1933 Paints ''Wounded Clown'' and ''Little Family,'' of which tapestries are made at the Aubusson works under the supervision of Madame Marie Cuttoli.
Mrs. Chester Dale donates a painting by Rouault to the Musée du Luxembourg, Paris—the first to figure in this museum.

1933 Matisse finishes his great mural decoration for Dr. Barnes at Merion, Pa.

1937 Large showing of his work (42 canvases) at the Petit-Palais in a room set aside for him at the exhibition ''Masters of Independent Art,'' held in conjunction with the Paris World's Fair.

1937 Picasso paints "Guernica" and does engravings for his "Songe et mensonge de Franco."

1938 Exhibition of Rouault prints at the Museum of Modern Art, New York.

1939 Death of Ambroise Vollard.

1940 Lionello Venturi publishes his first monograph on Rouault in New York (180 plates).

1940- Rouault retrospective exhibitions in Boston, Washington and
1941 San Francisco.

1945 Large Rouault retrospective at the Museum of Modern Art, New York. Canon Devemy and Father Couturier commission him to design five stained-glass windows for the church at Assy (Haute-Savoie), on which Bonnard, Matisse, Lurçat, Léger, Bazaine and Germaine Richier also collaborate. Two of these windows were executed by Hébert Stevens after Rouault's designs; the other three were made by Paul Bony after paintings chosen by Rouault.

1946 Braque-Rouault exhibition at the Tate Gallery, London.

1947 Rouault brings a lawsuit against the heirs of Ambroise Vollard for the recovery of nearly 800 unfinished, unsigned paintings. He won his suit and the pictures were returned to him, except for 119 which had already been sold.

1947 Death of Bonnard and Marquet.
Manessier designs stained-glass windows for the church at Les Bréseux (Doubs).

1948 November 5. Before witnesses Rouault burns 315 of the canvases restored to him. France sends 26 paintings and 12 prints by Rouault to the Venice Biennale. Large-scale Rouault retrospective (263 items) at the Kunsthaus, Zurich.
Publication of "Miserere."
Nominated honorary member of the Royal Academy of Belgium.
Travels to Switzerland and visits Italy for the first time (Venice, Florence, Rome, Assisi, Siena).

1949 Delivers his first designs for enamels to be executed in the monastic workshops of the Abbey of Ligugé.
Travels to Belgium and visits Holland for the first time.

1949 Matisse decorates the Dominican Chapel of Vence, on the Riviera, built to his own designs.

1951 June 6. For his 80th birthday a celebration is held in his honor at the Palais de Chaillot in Paris, organized by the Centre Catholique des Intellectuels Français, and Abbé Morel gives the first showing of his film on Rouault's "Miserere."
Promoted Commander of the Legion of Honor.

1951 Léger designs stained-glass windows for the church at Audincourt (Doubs).

1952 Rouault retrospective exhibitions at the Palais des Beaux-Arts, Brussels, the Stedelijk Museum, Amsterdam, and the Musée National d'Art Moderne, Paris.

1953 Rouault retrospectives at the Cleveland Museum of Art, the Museum of Modern Art, New York, the County Museum of Los Angeles, and in Tokyo and Osaka.
Named Commander of the Order of St. Gregory the Great by Pope Pius XII.

1954 Rouault retrospective at the Galleria d'Arte Moderna, Milan.

1955 Named Commander of the Order of the Italian Republic and member of the Academy of St. Luke of Rome.

1956 Rouault exhibition at the Musée Toulouse-Lautrec, Albi.

1957 With Rouault's approval, the Ateliers Plasse-Lecaisne make a tapestry after his "Holy Face," to be hung over the altar of the chapel of Hem (Nord); the rest of the chapel is to be decorated by Manessier.

1958 Death of Rouault in Paris on February 13.
By government decree he was given a state funeral.
In the course of the ceremony, which took place at the church of Saint-Germain-des-Prés, speeches were made by Abbé Morel and M. Billières, Minister of National Education, and a message from André Lhote, speaking in behalf of French artists, was read in conclusion.

THE PRENTICE CRAFTSMAN, 1925. MUSÉE D'ART MODERNE, PARIS.

INTRODUCTION

ONLY yesterday Rouault was still with us, a kindly, cordial presence, a friend among friends, in spite of his fits of temper. Now that he is no more, we see him differently; he looms large in retrospect, he was even greater than we thought, and we find ourselves wondering how it is that Rouault lived for fifty years in isolation, yet could impress his personality so deeply on the art life of our century.

To write about him at one time was like following in his footsteps, along the highways and byways of his painting, and sharing his solitude. It was galling to think that so fine an artist should be so little appreciated, that the circle of his admirers should be so small, that he should be virtually unknown to the public at large and unpatronized either by the Church or by the French Government. It is true that the large exhibition of his works at the Petit-Palais in 1937, during the Paris World's Fair, was a revelation. But a barrier of hostility and indifference remained and anyone who took an interest in him became, as it were, his confederate.

Rouault's estrangement from the art world was due in large part to Ambroise Vollard, who provided the painter with a comfortable income but monopolized his entire production and jealously guarded it from prying eyes. Vollard became his sole agent about 1917. Thereafter the only paintings by Rouault in general circulation were those executed before the First World War, so that the appearance of his recent work at the 1937 exhibition created a sensation. The policy adopted by Vollard, however, is not the whole story. By the very nature of his art and his own temperament, Rouault was an independent, an outsider. Such had not always been the case, for in his youth he was the favorite pupil of Gustave Moreau and friendly with Matisse, his classmate in Moreau's studio; he played an active part, along with Matisse, Bonnard and others, in founding the Salon d'Automne in 1903 and exhibited there with the Fauves in 1905, though he was never a member of the group.

But all this was ancient history. As time went on and his art took shape and developed, he came to stand alone. Today it is easy to see what he owed both to the art of his time and to an older tradition of French painting. Daumier, Cézanne, Degas and Toulouse-Lautrec were his mentors and immunized him against that idealized academicism in which Gustave Moreau drilled him. Hence his sympathy for the Fauves. He himself initiated a variety of French expressionism in reaction against the Schools and as a gesture of solidarity with the religious revival in France which, at the turn of the century, so greatly influenced social conditions and moral standards.

Yet it was above all his character and cast of mind—perhaps the inherent greatness of the man—which came to isolate him from his contemporaries. It was Daumier and Courbet who secularized French painting, who made it independent of religion. Sacred art continued to exist, of course; sacred subjects continued to be treated. But it was not an art in which religious sentiment inspires and conditions the artist. For a time Rouault too submitted to the routines of sacred art, but from 1903 on his religious inspiration was a creative force enlisted in the service not only of revolutionary form but also of moral reform. Here was a phenomenon that had not been seen for a century or more.

Rouault exhibited with the Fauves in 1905, but it was obvious that he was not one of them. Instead of glorifying color, he made a liberal use of black to express his moods of anger and revolt. More than twenty years had to elapse before the full beauty of his colors blazed out. Not that his vehement paintings might be taken for a form of caricature; on the contrary, though they are polemical, almost belligerent works, with an epic sweep and power, they were never aimed at individuals, but at institutions, at the bourgeoisie, at social injustice, at prostitution [1]. The controversial character of Rouault's early work possesses an abstract value that caricatures do not possess.

It is an interesting point that Apollinaire classified Rouault among the Cubists. This was a mistake, but we can sympathize with the perplexity of Apollinaire, who discerned in Rouault's work a revolutionary departure in some respects parallel to that of the Cubists, though it belonged to another world.

Afterwards Rouault was attracted neither to Futurism, German Expressionism, Abstractionism, nor Surrealism. He made his own revolution, and in so doing laid the basis of his self-imposed isolation. Think of Matisse; how tactfully he kept in touch with the tendencies of his time, assimilating something from all yet always remaining himself, even in the last years when he fell under the spell of abstract art. Of Rouault, however, it may be said that from 1905 on he followed his own path, indifferent to what was going on around him. Yet he remains a living force in art, because his one-man revolution had quite as much vitality and power as the collective revolutions of his contemporaries. Indeed, his book illustrations and his expressionist style of painting, together with his handling of color in such natural conjunction with form, constitute a major contribution to the art heritage of our civilization.

Such, in brief, were the outward circumstances that conditioned Rouault's "isolationism," but they do not explain it. The only explanation is to be found in the man himself, in his spiritual outlook and his spiritual needs. The meditations Rouault published in 1944 under the title *Soliloques* [2] reveal the moral tenor of his solitude.

"Avoid giving lessons, since your own rather precarious judgment has so often to be revised. Don't turn away from your own time, out of spite, and don't always be defending yourself in pointless polemics, simply because you aren't in constant sympathy with your contemporaries, even though they may set less store by you than by a pebble in the road. " [3]

"Why should the work of art always be in keeping, in harmony with, an extension of, its time, its milieu, its meridian? Why not also in reaction now and then against its time, milieu, meridian, and a highly individual confession?" [4]

Today of course we know that Rouault belonged to his time precisely because he revolted against it. His revolt, however, was of a very special kind. In 1937 he wrote: "I am submissive, but revolt lies within the reach of all comers. It is harder to submit in silence to an inner summons and to spend one's life searching for means of expression which are sincere and suited to our temperament and our gifts, if we have any." [5]

Rouault has his roots in tradition, undoubtedly, but which tradition? "There exists a Tradition of painting, alive and admirable, not shriveled and withered like dried flowers. It is like an enduring perfume. Tradition does not mean School. I have no objection to admitting that it might mean that, but definitively, by no means! The play of life's hidden forces rules it out. " [6]

Rouault did not specify what that tradition is, and probably he would have been hard put to it to do so. Unorthodox criticism, by its very concern for objectivity, develops on lines that cannot help branching out into uncertainty.

"Popular art, you have lived your life far from the Institutes; otherwise would you still be alive? The School being anything but strong, though not dead—but not knowing in which direction to turn or whom to swear by. Nature imitation having failed to free it from a snobbish infatuation with Ingres, accusing some of being very modern and up-to-date, too responsive to success when they haven't courted it, troubled times in which strong doctrines make no headway and they think that after all it would be such a delight to taste of this success in competition with the next man, however ephemeral it is. In both camps, an occasional act of heroism, albeit not always very visible, each one drawing up his secret plans and seeking his own way, sometimes divided against himself but swaggering anyhow. This dream of youth of being faithful to an austere ideal, sometimes a little too high, a little too far from the gifts granted you—who can say that he has fully lived up to it?" [7]

True, the various handicrafts still constitute a living tradition. " One begins as a craftsman; one becomes an artist if one can. But is it not better to be a good craftsman than a bad artist? Here is one aspect of the modern problem."[8]

Rouault inherited from his father the craftsman's respect and love for his tools and materials. Rouault senior was a finisher and varnisher of pianos at the Pleyel factory in Paris. The creaking of a door irritated him, not because it made a noise, but because it indicated that the wood was "suffering" under a strain. The same sensibility made his son irritable in the presence of two discordant colors.

The habits of the workshop, the tradition of painstaking craftsmanship into which he was initiated in boyhood, account for his meticulous methods of work. His paintings are highly finished works on which he lavished infinite pains. If they often give the very opposite impression, the reason is that in the end the inventive genius of the artist got the upper hand of the craftsman's diligence.

The nature of his craftsmanship, moreover, changed with the years. Before 1903 he concentrated on achieving purity of line; in the last years of his life he was wholly concerned with superimposed layers of color. But the moral imperative behind his efforts was always the same: devotion to his work. His scruples about this were such that at times they may seem to have done more harm than good; several works, for example, which the present author admired and published in his two previous books on Rouault now no longer exist, having been either transformed out of recognition or destroyed. This trait of character is part and parcel of Rouault's congenital humility, which he retained to the full even when he finally became a world-famous figure. His abiding sense of humility toward his art was the same which bowed him humbly before God.

Underlying all the sentiments and all the actions of Rouault's life was his faith. It was more than a deep-seated belief or creed; it was a pure, unswerving faith, austere, Jansenistic, even cruel on occasion, and bound up with the strictest moral austerity. If he sometimes seemed hard of heart in his dealings with others, he spared himself even less; in this he went to heroic lengths. To this he owed his force, his spiritual detachment, his certitude, both in life and art. He was familiar with anguish but not with doubt; troubled spirits invariably subsided into peace of mind. With Rouault the technical ideals of the craftsman were inseparable from his faith: he worshipped the perfection of God's works. The creative artist in him felt humble before his own creations.

In his search for the fitting artistic expression of his faith, Rouault went through some dramatic phases. Before 1903, when he had not yet freed himself from academic form, he expressed his religious feelings in terms of physical beauty. During this period he practised sacred art of a kind which, as it happened, was also a commercial success; everyone delighted in his angels. After 1903 he was in no mood for angels; his eyes had been opened to the sordid side of life, to the triumph of vice and ugliness. He suspected himself of hypocrisy in painting angels, of glossing over the evils of the world, of suppressing the truth. For his faith to remain intact he had to wage war on evil. Not angels but prostitutes were now the subject of his pictures, and the image of Christ as the divinely appointed victim of man's violence and cruelty to man. In the end his triumph was complete. But who will ever be able to tell how much this radical change of direction cost young Rouault? This much is certain, however: in order to save his faith he became the knight of a one-man crusade.

His expert craftsmanship never lapsed into virtuosity, his religious zeal never led him to confuse art and propaganda— and this for a very simple reason. Rouault was a man of the people. Born and bred in the workaday environment of artisans who earn their daily bread with their own hands, he never lost touch with the home truths of life as it is lived by the working classes, even when he had acquired the broader culture associated with higher levels in the social scale. Claude Roulet, who has made an interesting study of Rouault's character as revealed in his writings, has this to say: "Rouault's style follows the spoken language of the people. Like the vernacular, it is racy, natural, direct, colorful. Though it is simple, by which I mean cursory, clear, colloquial, it is by no means easy to describe. The reason is that this style is original, and that, among all the forms of originality, it is the vivid expression of a complex nature...

"Instinctively he chose the way of speaking best suited to his nature: that of the common people who live in the street. The idiom of the open air, not of cafés or small hotel-rooms. The idiom of the heart of Paris." [9]

The pictures painted between 1903 and 1918 testify to his sympathy with popular ways, with the open streets, and the warmth of that sympathy tempers and mitigates the acerbity of his social criticism and moral indictments. Sometimes, as in *Circus Parade*, his lightness of touch prevails over his powerful volumes. It is not too much to say that Rouault's sympathy with the common people served as a safety valve against the excesses of his zeal. A case in point is the *Portrait of Mr. X.* The curators of the Museum of Modern Art in New York pressed him to reveal the identity of the model. At last Rouault replied: it was the portrait of no one in particular, it was an imaginary figure. This seemed incredible, for the portrait has all the conviction, all the intensity of an actual encounter. Yet it was true: Rouault had succeeded in giving form to the features of a type figure for which he felt a kind of sentimental fellowship. It is, moreover, too sincere and honest a type to represent the despised bourgeois.

Attributing it to Daumier, Rouault gave an excellent definition of his own attitude toward the bourgeois, "whom he blames neither for his hardheartedness nor for the unconscious selfishness that lurks beneath his pretence of affability, but rather for his priggish conviction that he makes the world go round and secures our well-being by looking after his own. Comic and grotesque were it not that, under a cloak of almost priestlike candor, he presumes to judge us all." [10]

To run its course, the vehemence of Rouault's paintings needed the admixture of an element to be found not in the art but in the literature of the nineties. That element was personified by Alfred Jarry. Remove every vestige of intelligence from the object of your moral censure: all you have left is a fierce boor named Ubu and the pitiless animality of the "supermale." The farther you go in ridding an evil-doer of the pangs of conscience, the more you have to magnify the evil done, making it a force of nature in order to justify your reaction to it. This explains why it has been said of Rouault that his reaction to social evils is truly a "catastrophic deliverance."

The catastrophe is interpreted, however, on lines that are fanciful rather than realistic—just as Jarry prescribed, in fact. The moral crusade becomes an artistic crusade by virtue of the aspiration to an ideal way of life: that of the clown.

In his book *Le Cirque de l'Etoile Filante* (1938) Rouault touches on his early sufferings, the reasons for his revolt, and his adventures in the art world. He recalls his childhood and the escapes he made from the hardships of daily life. "Dream or reality: even had the pale child of the suburbs not wandered into the big tent of the Shooting Star Circus, sidling toward it or making straight for it, still as he grew older would he have found other pretexts for forgetting the long winters, the joyless days, the hard or hostile masks of the dispirited and the withered of heart." [11]

Clowns were the dream of Rouault's life. For them he reserved those accents of naïve admiration which, early on, turned into a storm of imprecation against everything else. "Strolling players over all the highways of Ile-de-France, drifting from North to South, from East to West, fun-loving, peace-making conquerors who go your way in winter toward the sun, the green plain in spring or toward the ocean sea, I have always envied you, I a recluse tilling the pictorial soil as the peasant tills his field, now toward Spain you go by way of Navarre, now toward Flanders—all at once making off for the Straits of Gibraltar, moving forward at less than 300 an hour—good old shuffling Rosinante, far from the Venturers of the Celestial Highways; from the consortiums of the Mad Match King, whose matches catch on indistinctly at both ends or not at all; from the garglings of pettifogging classicists, or the latest agents of clandestine armaments for World Peace; near the Cape of Good Hope or the Bay of Departed Souls." [12]

Rouault painted many clowns in the course of his life, and even went so far as to lend them the features of his own face. Circus life of course had inspired many artists before him; suffice it to mention Seurat and Toulouse-Lautrec. But Rouault struck a new note: his heart went out to the clowns, he envied them the nomadic life they led, with their finger, as it were, forever on the popular pulse, practising an unproblematical art. They are craftsmen of the best type by virtue of the elemental appeal of their art; their voice is the voice of the people.

There were no flowers of rhetoric in the popular soil in which Rouault sank his roots. And into his figure paintings, however "grotesque" or "distorted," there never crept that streak of arrogance or superiority so common to caricature. Baudelaire drew the distinction applicable here: "The comic, from the artistic point of view, is an imitation; the grotesque is a creation... I shall hereafter call the grotesque absolute comedy, in contradistinction to ordinary comedy, which I shall call significant comedy." [13] The grotesque, in other words, may be said to have formal coherence, and is therefore art, whereas caricature merely accentuates the naturalistic relationships which stand in the way of that organization of forms which alone deserves the name of art. Rouault's satirical figures are absolute grotesques; such is the *Portrait of Mr. X*, it is not a caricature. In the paintings of clowns Rouault's sarcastic outbursts against the vices and vileness of society have given place to equanimity. So it is that today, when in many cases we fail to respond to the urgency of Rouault's violence, we can always appreciate the art which that violence gave rise to.

Another remarkable trait of character, quite unexpected in an artist of Rouault's caliber, was his keen legal sense; here indeed, in the turning of legal quibbles to his own advantage, he carried shrewdness to the point of cunning, and prided himself on doing so. In 1943 he wrote in *Le Point*: "I sometimes dream, in these last years of my life, of upholding a thesis at the Sorbonne on the spiritual defense of works of art and the artist's rights before the law, and the ways and means of securing these rights, so that those who come after us may be better protected, to this effect—the end in view not being exclusively material or selfish, but above all a spiritual right which should be conceded to the creator of a body of painted or engraved work in his lifetime and even after his death."

In 1947, in the highly charged atmosphere of Paris after the Liberation, Rouault realized his dream to an extent that surpassed his expectations. He was not asked to uphold a thesis at the Sorbonne, but he won his lawsuit against the heirs of Ambroise Vollard and thus recovered nearly 800 unsigned, unfinished paintings in their possession—works which he, as their author, considered unworthy to be sold under his name. No one but the artist himself has the right to decide whether one of his works should or should not appear before the public. Here was a principle whose importance far transcended the case of Rouault *versus* Vollard Heirs; it was a momentous step toward the legal recognition of the artist's spiritual rights.

Rouault's personality was rich and complex; the analyst who attempts to fathom it will have his work cut out for him. Such is not our task here. It seemed necessary, however, to recall briefly the early background of his career and the circumstances and grievances which led him to isolate himself. The social crusade to which he committed himself was, moreover, the consequence, not the origin, of his character, of his religious faith, of his training as a craftsman, of his sympathy for the people, of his evasion toward sarcasm and satire. These are the ever-recurring features of a career that spanned over half a century.

HEAD OF A TRAGIC CLOWN, 1904.
BANGERTER COLLECTION, MONTREUX.

24

APPRENTICESHIP AND REVOLT

GEORGES ROUAULT inherited an indelible trait of character that ran in the family: the tenacity and scrupulousness of the artisan. He was born in the Belleville district of Paris, 51, rue de la Villette, near Père Lachaise Cemetery, on May 27, 1871, during the insurrection of the Commune. On that very day government troops under Marshal MacMahon captured Belleville, the Red Republican quarter of the city, and the gunfire and cannonading of civil war probably hastened his mother's confinement. At birth the child was so small, so puny, that he was not expected to live, but his health improved at the Belleville home of his maternal grandfather, Champdavoine. In afteryears Rouault retained the memory of his grandfather's admiration for Manet. His aunts painted fans and chinaware, and as a child he often amused himself with their colors.

His father was a native of Montfort, in Brittany; a cabinet-maker by trade, he worked at the Pleyel piano factory. He was a fervent admirer of Lamennais, and when the activities of that great Catholic democrat were publicly condemned by the pope, he turned against the Church and sent his son to a Protestant school. As a result, however, of too severe a punishment in class, he removed the boy and had him apprenticed to a stained-glass maker. Young Rouault's second employer was Georges Hirsch, a restorer of old stained glass, who made the windows for the church of Saint-Séverin (in Paris) while Rouault was working in his studio. Albert Besnard invited him to collaborate on the stained-glass windows he had designed for the Ecole de Pharmacie; but Rouault refused, out of loyalty to Hirsch. In this attitude there was something of the naïve code of honor which children observe amongst themselves; all his life Rouault remained childlike, in the best sense of the word, in spite of the "bad temper" on which too much stress has been laid.

The thick black contours and juxtaposed planes of pure colors characteristic of Rouault's later paintings have been accounted for by his early training as a stained-glass painter. But this is a gross simplification. Examine the windows in the church of Saint-Séverin; it will be seen that they have nothing in common with Rouault's style. It is only fair to note, however, that he was greatly impressed by examples of 13th-century stained glass which came to Hirsch's studio for mending. Rouault wrote to me as follows of some of the things he saw there.

"I have had the opportunity, luckily for me, of examining restorations of medieval stained glass as they passed through my hands. It was brought home to me then how low the art of the stained-glass maker, like that of the tapestry weaver, had fallen—mere imitations of bad oil paintings by people in many cases highly respected and even famous. And this *staggered* me, though I was only a child at the time; I was fourteen when I started. To give you an example: I saw mere chromolithographs on glossy paper slipped between two panes of leaded glass. The reaction against this sort of thing has taken time, it has taken half a century... It is possible to start out as an artisan and develop into a sensitive artist little by little, step by step, without taking oneself for a born classic or a genius."

The juxtaposed zones of color typical of his mature style are no doubt an echo of his early training. All the same, however, Rouault's thick black contours have an essentially pictorial value. They do not perform the technical function of binding the color surfaces, like the strips of lead in a stained-glass window; they perform the artistic function of bringing out the colors by contrast, of making them sing. Not the recollection of the great cathedral windows or his apprenticeship with a glass painter but the working habits of sound craftsmanship, learned in his father's house, account for the unhurried steadiness and self-dedication with which he always carried out his work.

While still working as a glass painter, Rouault attended evening classes at the Ecole des Arts Décoratifs. All his life he kept in his studio a drawing from a plaster cast, made there in 1886, and a study from the living model, made in 1890.

In 1891 he enrolled in Elie Delaunay's studio at the Ecole des Beaux-Arts. When this teacher died a few months later, he was succeeded by Gustave Moreau, who discerned Rouault's gifts and took a special interest in him. As early as July 1892, with a series of religious subjects, Rouault won the *prix d'atelier*, which usually went to a senior member of the class. In 1894 he was awarded the Prix Chenavard for *The Child Jesus among the Doctors*. In 1895 he won the Prix Fortin d'Ivry and an award at the Salon. As early as 1893, at the urging of Gustave Moreau, he competed for the Prix de Rome with *Samson at the Mill*, but was unsuccessful. He competed again in 1895 with *Christ mourned by the Holy Women*, and when this too was unsuccessful Moreau advised him to leave the school. He always considered Rouault his best pupil and even gave him material assistance.

In 1898 Moreau died and Rouault, the spiritual heir of the master, became curator of the Musée Gustave Moreau. Half a century later Rouault still spoke of him with the same veneration, with the same sympathy and cordiality, as if Moreau were still living, and as if Rouault himself were still a raw youth at the feet of a mentor whose judgments he trusted implicitly both in art and in life. The most moving pages of Rouault's *Souvenirs Intimes* (1926) are those devoted to Moreau.

Put Moreau's paintings beside those of Rouault, however, and it will be seen that they represent two different temperaments, two different worlds, two different civilizations. For one thing, Moreau never departed from the canons of academic draftsmanship, while Rouault's work is its very antithesis. Moreau never explored the possibilities of color but shrouded it in Rembrandtesque shadows, while Rouault carried chromatic intensity to its highest pitch. One aspired to an ideal beauty and deliberately avoided the interpretation of reality; the other plunged to the very roots of the most squalid realities of daily life. As human beings, too, the two men were utterly different. Rouault's attachment to the Christian faith was deep-seated and intuitive; he was a servant of the Absolute, never reasoning, never drawing fine distinctions, but simply believing. Moreau was an intellectual, admitting the existence of God with a certain detachment due to a kind of moral respect for the unknowable. Far from being a rebel, Moreau was a man who, after tasting success and fame, fell back upon his inmost self with an aristocratic revulsion from passing fashions and artistic speculation. Rouault was always giving battle. He burnt all his bridges behind him, and it might even be said that with him the expression of affection took the form of an imprecation.

What did young Rouault learn from Gustave Moreau for him to be so devoted to the memory of his master half a century later, in a world so much changed that Moreau's very name is practically forgotten?

Think of the admiration and affection a Christian like Dante always felt for the Stoics. In his *Souvenirs Intimes* Rouault gives us not a literal portrait of Gustave Moreau but the sketch of an almost legendary figure: the image of a great Stoic. The aloofness, the non-committal reserve of the master, appeared to the pupil as the outward apanage of a hidden truth endowed with limitless power thanks to the mystery in which it shrouded itself. The picture we get is that of an academic painter capable not only of loving his pupil but of appreciating him for gifts very different from, even opposed to, his own. In a word, Moreau taught in a wholly liberal spirit. He was unprejudiced enough to discern all that was false and artificial in academic instruction. He was not a rebel, but he was a dissenter. He had no hesitation about visiting the Salon des Indépendants and could appreciate what he saw there—to the great disgust of his colleagues. At the same time he did his best to keep his pupils independent of the fashions of the day: Impressionism, Neo-Impressionism, Symbolism, and other schools. These he regarded, nevertheless, with tolerance and respect. He preferred Claude Lorrain to Corot, but he appreciated Corot.

To the triumphant realism of that day Moreau opposed not an academic set of rules but the imaginative powers of the mind and the impetus of high spiritual aspirations. In this he was a belated romantic, but to an inexperienced youth this effete romanticism easily assumed the guise of an idealism foreshadowing the new tendencies of the 20th century, and containing, as it were, the seeds of Surrealism.

The fact is that the idealism of Moreau's painting and the liberalism of his teaching prepared the way not only for Rouault but also for Matisse, his fellow student in Moreau's class. With his naïve, forthright, religious, imaginative turn of mind, it was only natural for Rouault to find in the affection of his teacher and in his outstanding qualities both as a man and a professor the moral support he needed to develop his own personality. So it was that he came to identify with Moreau everything that finally blossomed out of that affection.

Even apart from this, it was to Moreau that Rouault owed not only his absolute mastery of academic draftsmanship but also, and above all, his abiding interest in everything that transcends matter and natural appearances. This preoccupation with the spiritual significance of things became so imperative, so absorbing, that for Rouault it merged with reality itself.

For some time after leaving the Ecole des Beaux-Arts he tried out various approaches to a personal style. There are early sketches whose delicacy and precision recall the silverpoint drawings of this or that Old Master, and early paintings indebted to the luminism of Seurat, to the Dutch landscapists and, most

TRAGIC CLOWN, 1903.
WATERCOLOR. HAHNLOSER COLLECTION, BERN.

of all perhaps, to Rembrandt. It was still an art of undigested fragments culled from the museums, and though there are personal touches amid a variety of tendencies, there is as yet little or no sign of genuine creative power.

The strong religious strain that ran through his art to the very end was already manifest in his student years. His preference went to sacred subjects; indeed he specialized at first in sacred art and made a success of it, finding dealers who were eager to purchase his production. But it was sacred, not religious art. In spite of the quality of the execution, it was the subject that counted, it was the more or less traditional imagery that justified the picture. For it to become religious art there had to be a new form, peculiarly his own, in which to convey the religious sentiment.[14] And to achieve this there had to be an inner revolution; this in fact took place from 1903 on.

When Rouault left the museums and went down into the streets, he recorded daily life chiefly in the persons of clowns and prostitutes, whom he painted in forms unexampled in his earlier manner: such are *Prostitutes* (1903), *Head of a Tragic Clown* (1904), *Prostitute* (1906), *Prostitute before a Mirror* (1906), *Odalisque* (1907). Though it was an abrupt change of style, actually it had been in the making for some time, both artistically and morally.

While still a student Rouault had asked permission to go down to the South of France and paint from nature, following the example of Cézanne, but Moreau had advised him against it. After his master's death in 1898, Rouault reverted to the idea; he went out and painted some landscapes in the open air and so learned to relate the volume of objects to the general effect of light and shadow. Above all, his study of Cézanne encouraged him to render form boldly without the aid of academic formulas, and impressed him with the need for a coherent unity of the picture elements above and beyond any reference to visual reality. His conception of space changed accordingly; instead of being locked in a closed space, his figures came to occupy a limitless, self-contained, imaginary space. Thus Rouault, at about the same time as the Fauves, created for himself the same conditions of imaginative freedom in the handling of form that they did. Fittingly enough, he exhibited with the Fauves, though he never belonged to the group.

This change of style went hand in hand with a change of his religious outlook. It is a matter of record that in the last decade of the 19th century a resurgence of religious life took place in France. Before 1903, as already noted, Rouault had painted pictures on sacred themes, that is, works of religious imagery, little different from those of many other painters. Not till after 1903 was his faith kindled and intensified sufficiently for him to embark on a crusade against moral corruption and social evils. What is remarkable is that, except for a few heads of Christ, his subject matter ceased to be sacred, ceased to be biblical, at the very time when his art became genuinely religious. Why was this so?

Rouault had met J. K. Huysmans in 1901, after the novelist's conversion to Catholicism. Huymans was a great admirer of Gustave Moreau. But he was a dilettante in matters of religious art, a man of refined tastes on the look-out for an ivory tower in which to go on dreaming undisturbed. His temperament was not virile enough to have any shaping influence on the exceptionally energetic nature of young Rouault.

Very different were the consequences of his meeting with the writer Léon Bloy. A devout Catholic, Bloy did not know what it was to doubt. His philosophy began and ended with the Christian faith. He always spoke on behalf of the Absolute. He made no allowance for the infinite scale of conditions and tempers that differentiates human beings; hence, very often, the inhumanity of the man. In his obsession with the Absolute he condemned the world around him *en bloc*, without distinguishing between good and evil, without giving anyone or anything a fair trial. And when the reaction against him came, on the part of churchmen, men of letters and politicians alike, Bloy abused and insulted them all so indiscriminately that he often confused God's interests with his own. Still, his sincerity cannot be questioned, nor his greatness as a defender of the faith and

PROSTITUTES, 1903. WATERCOLOR. HAHNLOSER COLLECTION, BERN.

upholder of God's rights on earth. His tremendous force of persuasion lay in his unshakable convictions, in his extremism, in his wrathful denunciation of the hypocrisy that inevitably flourishes in every organized religion.

Neither the Counter-Reformation nor the romantic Catholicism of the Nazarenes nor the Neo-Catholicism of the late 19th century succeeded in creating the climate necessary for a rebirth of religious art, because each fixed a limited practical objective for itself—a political and social objective. A return had to be made to the fountainhead of religious faith, the springs of that primitive faith had to be tapped, contact with a God anterior to Satan had to be made, in order for a new faith to be generated and to become again a spontaneous emotion and an absolute necessity of life. This was the work of Léon Bloy, and he carried it out in spite of all his shortcomings. It was only natural for a deeply, vehemently religious-minded man like Rouault, inclined by nature to extremes of apocalyptic imprecation, to find in Léon Bloy not simply a friend but an elder brother.

Léon Bloy stood not for Christian civilization but for Christian barbarism. He railed furiously against "honest folk, who are nothing but soft and sticky monsters, equally incapable of the abominations of vice and the abominations of virtue."

The abomination of vice, expiation through suffering, depths of abjection in atonement for sin—these things were always uppermost in Bloy's mind. In his novel *La Femme pauvre*, published in 1897 before he met Rouault, Bloy had a prophetic vision of a painter who in many ways resembles the Rouault of later years. The character's name is Lazare Druide. "He is a painter, this fellow, just as he might be a lion or a shark, an earthquake or a deluge, because it is absolutely necessary to be what God wills and nothing else... But painting, or, if you like, the syntax of painting, its precepts and methods, its laws, canons, rubrics, dogmas, liturgy, tradition, nothing of this has ever crossed his doorstep... Like Delacroix, he is blamed for the slovenliness of his drawing and the furor of his color. He is blamed most of all for existing, for he is really too full of life.

His fellow artists, with their sluggish imaginations, find it hard to account for such impetuous bursts of life. How could he possibly linger over minute details in the execution of his pictures, even if such rigorous accuracy were indispensable? Do they not see that by hanging back he might never catch up again with his inspired spirit, as it scampers ahead, unbridled and unchecked?... That spirit of his is all he has, the most generous and princely of spirits! He seizes upon it, dips it, steeps it in a subject worthy of it and flings it, shimmering, on to the canvas! That is the whole extent of his technique... but so great is its power that a cry goes up, there is wailing and sobbing and a rush for the exit, with arms thrown up in amazement!

"Such was the phenomenon that occurred at the exhibition of his *Andronicus delivered up to the Populace of Byzantium.*"

Everything preceding the mention of the picture title is wonderfully prophetic, but that title spoils it all. The only way for Lazare Druide (i.e. Rouault) to attain perfection, to be true to himself, was to paint not the history of Byzantium, but the first wretch he met in the street. Here was the flaw, here was the prophet's delusion—which explains Bloy's complete failure to understand Rouault.

In his diary for March 16, 1904, he noted Rouault's enthusiasm for *La Femme pauvre.* "My book has touched him to the quick, and left a wound that will never heal. I tremble to think of the sufferings in store for the unfortunate man." On May 1, 1905, Bloy visited the Musée Gustave Moreau where Rouault's early academic work, *The Child Jesus among the Doctors* (1894), was exhibited. "I didn't realize that Rouault had an immense talent. I realize it now and have told him so enthusiastically." But then, on October 31, 1905, he saw Rouault's latest works at the Salon d'Automne. "It's a sorry sight. He's seeking a new path, what a pity! This artist apparently capable of painting the angels now does nothing else but the most shocking and

PROSTITUTE, 1906. WATERCOLOR AND PASTEL.
PETIT-PALAIS, PARIS.

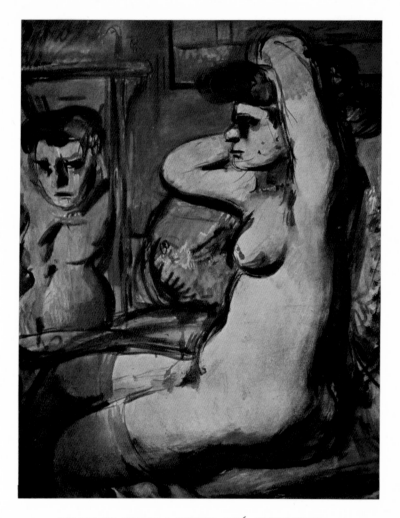

PROSTITUTE BEFORE A MIRROR, 1906. WATERCOLOR.
MUSÉE D'ART MODERNE, PARIS.

BATHERS, 1907. WATERCOLOR.
PHILIPPE LECLERCQ COLLECTION, HEM.

vindictive caricatures. Bourgeois foulness has wrought so violent and horrified a reaction in him that his art seems to have received the death blow." On May 1, 1907, after visiting the Salon, he sat down and wrote to Rouault as follows. "Naturally I saw your one and only, sempiternal canvas, forever the same slut or the same clown, with this single, lamentable difference that, each time, the scum seems to increase... I have two things to say to you today, after which you will be no more to me than a friendly carcass. First: you are attracted exclusively by the ugly, your head is swimming with hideous sights.

ODALISQUE, 1907. WATERCOLOR. BANGERTER COLLECTION, MONTREUX.

Second: if you were a man of prayer and obedience, if you were a thanks-giver, you would be incapable of painting these horrible canvases. A Rouault capable of depth would feel slightly terror-stricken."

Because he had the courage to follow his calling as an artist, Rouault pushed on straight ahead and had no more artistic dealings with Léon Bloy. Yet they remained friends. Bloy sent his books to Rouault with affectionate dedications, and Rouault continued to call on him till Bloy's death in 1917.

To understand how it was that Bloy could analyse Rouault's art so rightly and judge it so wrongly, it is well to remember that Bloy, writing on December 14, 1915, described Cézanne as "the most lamentable of artists" because he failed to "render" what he saw. Now for Bloy, as for so many others, to "render" meant to give a painting that smooth academic finish which Cézanne called *"le fini des imbéciles."* Rouault, as a matter of fact, rendered to perfection the loathing for bourgeois life which he felt so deeply, and which to some extent had been due to the influence of Bloy himself. In expressing this revulsion of feeling he achieved a certain lyrical and tragic grandeur. Unable to comply at the same time with Bloy's wishes and with his own, Rouault not unreasonably chose to go his own way.

He was in no mood for painting angels. Religious conviction with him had nothing to do with transcendent dreams. It was a reaction against the society he lived in, and a way out of the prison-house of crime and ugliness to which his eyes had been opened. To understand the tradition with which, at this stage, Rouault's art linked up, we must go back to the late 18th-century idea of a "characteristic" as opposed to "ideal beauty" —an idea which found fulfillment in caricature. It chiefly served moral and political ends, but it was also an end in itself and offered a fertile field for artists at a time when so many traditional themes had been sterilized by the convention of the *beau idéal*.

The first hero of this new tendency was Goya, with—wrote Baudelaire—"his love of the elusive and indefinable, his feeling for violent contrasts, for the terrors of nature and for human faces strangely bestialized by circumstances. The great merit of Goya consists in making the monstrous convincing. His monsters are born viable and harmonic. No one has dared more than he in the way of rendering the absurd probable. All these contortions, these bestial faces, these diabolical grimaces, are steeped in humanity." [15]

It was a long way from Goya to Daumier. Between them stood Romanticism, for which the "comic" was only the sublime turned inside out. Caricature came to express a democratic familiarity, a new sense of generosity, indeed of fellow feeling. The art of Daumier is the consequence, expressed in terms of caricature, of his reaction against society; at the same time, he represents the liberation of the artist.

With neither Goya nor Daumier was distortion a laughing matter. Goya distorted to give vent to his anger; Daumier, to evince the pity he felt for human suffering and human weakness. There is a tragic side to all their "comic" figures.

Nor does Toulouse-Lautrec make us laugh, on the contrary. His incisive, broken line serves to build up his defense against humanity: the defense of one who feels himself an outcast from his own class and milieu because of an infirmity, a physical anomaly. If perchance an accent of pity or even of awakened sympathy creeps into his work, it comes only as the subdued accompaniment of an indifference willfully imposed by pride.

Neither Daumier nor Toulouse-Lautrec manifests any of Rouault's exasperation. The first is too humane, the second too much of an aristocrat, to throw himself into the fray as Rouault did. Both, moreover, while modifying it, always retained a respect for traditional forms which Rouault had ceased to feel. Even when compared with Goya's most violent outbursts,

Rouault's work introduces something new and unexpected: a religious consciousness which magnifies the scope of the indictment and makes it more severe.

Rouault's change of style occurred abruptly and with a facility that is reflected in the lightness of his touch. The *Prostitutes* of 1903 (Hahnloser Collection, Bern) is a watercolor built up in contrasts of light and shade within a picture space incompletely defined, intended not to contain the figures but to project them toward the spectator, with all the force of living presences. This might be likened to an impressionist technique, were it not that the solidity, the sheer bulk of the figures and the energy of their gestures, together with their expressive intensity, unmistakably belong to an altogether different world.

Head of a Tragic Clown (1904, Bangerter Collection, Montreux) is an extreme instance of those bursts of light flashing through utter darkness, out of which a ghostly figure looms, with no attempt to give it plastic definition and consistency. Yet the volumes of that figure are ample and firm, even though suggested by a technique apparently invented for the purpose of destroying volume. Forms are pressed to the brink of obscurity and disintegration as a means of intensifying the tragic expression of the clown, his rankling anger, and his resignation.

The 1904 Salon d'Automne was memorable for the pictures by Cézanne, Renoir and Toulouse-Lautrec exhibited there. It was largely as a result of this exhibition that the painters of the younger generation adopted Cézanne and Renoir as their masters. Rouault had shown only two pictures at the 1903 Salon d'Automne: *Paris, Grey Weather* and *Portrait Study*. At the 1904 Salon, however, he showed eight oil paintings and thirty-two watercolors and pastels; the oils were *Prostitute in a Red Dress, Clown, Clowness, Circus Sketch, Circus Girl Smoking, Acrobat in Yellow, Pierrot and his Family, Fat Woman*. Thus already in 1904 we are confronted with the themes that were to underlie

his work for the rest of his life. What had taken place was a
formal revolution in his approach to art and a moral revolution
in his outlook on life—a simultaneous occurrence indicative of
the organic unity of his artistic personality.

PARTY AT THE WATERSIDE, 1906. MADAME NETTER COLLECTION, PARIS.

HEAD OF CHRIST, 1905.
COLLECTION OF WALTER P. CHRYSLER, JR., NEW YORK.

At the 1905 Salon d'Automne Rouault exhibited only three pictures, but important works. One, entitled *Prostitutes*, was a kind of triptych, catalogued as follows: 1. *Monsieur et Madame Poulot, from "La Femme pauvre" by Léon Bloy* — 2. *Prostitute* — 3. *Terpsichore*. This allusion to Léon Bloy, at that time a controversial figure in the literary world of Paris, and the full maturity Rouault had now achieved in his "grotesque" style amply justified the heated reactions to which the artist gave rise in 1905. His work was abundantly represented at the Salon d'Automne for the next three years, and provided plenty of food for controversy and scandal, for it was a withering denunciation not only of the bogus conventions of society but of the pseudo-idealistic abstractions and embellishments of contemporary art. The works exhibited by Rouault seemed to hit the public square in the face, rousing them from their lethargy.

The directive principle of Rouault's new style is embodied in a *Head of Christ* (Collection of Walter P. Chrysler, Jr., New York) which repays study. The slashing strokes of the brush are always alongside the contour of a form and never coincide with it; they symbolize the shadows of contours. The image has become less distinct but more vividly alive: its spiritual energy has increased in proportion as its physical outlines have faded away. In many previous Heads of Christ the artist had respected the traditional contours of the figure, which had put a brake on his powers of expression. The same principle governs the color scheme, which is quite bright (sky blue, pink, and very light greens and yellows), though at the time Rouault's palette was habitually dark. But in this *Head of Christ* he resorted to bright colors in order to obtain tragic expression by contrast. The mood no longer coincides with the symbolic value of the colors, but contrasts with it. Lines and colors together are pressed into the service of a style expressive of "the other side of things." Every hint of material form or tangible plasticity disappears and, at the same time, chromatic expression becomes indirect. By the destruction of form Rouault obtains the form of the *terrible*, just as he obtains the expression of torture by means of colors which in themselves denote joy.

Here the question arises: what is the real moral content of this *Head of Christ*? The pity it expresses is too free, too fierce, to give rise to compassion. This is a revolt against the inhuman cruelty of which Christ was a victim, and the almost joyous impetus of revolt throws a veil of lyricism across this specter of cruelty and purges the picture of its latent brutality. The subject is Christ, but the motif is inverted: it is man's cruelty to man. Thus the style of "the other side," as embodied here in lines and colors, coincides perfectly with a manner of apprehending Christ which also belongs to "the other side of things."

In 1905, as noted, Rouault exhibited *Monsieur et Madame Poulot*. This is one of his greatest masterpieces. Painted in watercolors and gouache, with touches of India ink, it forms a calm harmony of blues and pinks, against which the figures stand out discreetly, without thrusting themselves upon us. All the more powerful, therefore, is the satirical emphasis on the vulgarity of the couple, who are deprived however of none of their humanity. Perhaps Léon Bloy's resentment was aroused by that very vulgarity, which mirrored his own imagination. To understand this object lesson in how to combine the satirical and the humane, we have to refer to what I have called "the style of the other side," in which, the less insistent he seems, the more intimately the painter reveals himself.

Clowns lent themselves admirably to the realization of this style, for it was a theme that allowed the artist to follow his fancy freely and to take full advantage of allusive signs, of flickering lights and shadows, which lose all precision of outline and play over the picture uncertainly and irrationally. *Conjurer* (1907, Madame Simon Collection, Paris) and *Circus Parade*

THE COUPLE (MONSIEUR ET MADAME POULOT), 1905.
WATERCOLOR AND GOUACHE. PHILIPPE LECLERCQ COLLECTION, HEM.

CIRCUS PARADE, 1907. WATERCOLOR AND PASTEL.
BANGERTER COLLECTION, MONTREUX.

(1907, Bangerter Collection, Montreux) are good examples of this manner. *Conjurer* is a masterpiece of lightness and luministic coherence, quite detached from the model, as if the artist were on the threshold of an art independent of nature. In *Circus Parade* stress is laid on the grotesque, so that the representation is more precise in spite of the vagaries of the brushwork. The dominant trend of Rouault's style was now to give concrete form to the signs indicative of the "other side," and to embody it in the grotesque, in castigations of the vices of society.

CONJURER, 1907. MADAME SIMON COLLECTION, PARIS.

The violence of Rouault's caricature bursts out in full force in two works: *Judges* (1908, Copenhagen) and *"Aunt Sallys"* or *The Bride*, exhibited at the 1907 Salon d'Automne and now in the Tate Gallery, London. These figures are full-fledged monsters, denizens of Erebus, loosed on the world to spread scurrility, rebellion and panic. Daumier before him had represented repulsive judges and Toulouse-Lautrec hardened prostitutes, but Rouault's approach was different. His monsters

JUDGES, 1908. ROYAL MUSEUM OF FINE ARTS, COPENHAGEN.

have a kind of natural grandeur which lifts them to a higher plane. And this effect stems from the crusading anger that moves him to indignation and reproof. When he paints clowns, however, then the grotesque becomes amiable, even lovable, as in the *Pierrot* of 1910 (Collection of Joseph Pulitzer, Jr., St. Louis) where colors grow rich and resplendent, almost as if the artist, laying aside his crusader's arms for a moment, were relaxing in the light of the sun and letting it flood into his work.

"AUNT SALLYS" OR THE BRIDE, 1907. TATE GALLERY, LONDON.

PIERROT, 1910.
COLLECTION OF MR. AND MRS. JOSEPH PULITZER, JR., ST. LOUIS.

PORTRAIT OF MR. X, 1911.
ALBRIGHT-KNOX ART GALLERY, BUFFALO, N.Y.

The *Portrait of Mr. X* (Albright-Knox Art Gallery, Buffalo), as noted, is not an actual portrait; it is the synthesis of Rouault's style, or rather of the variations of style which we have seen up to this point. The synthesis is so complete, however, that an imaginary figure acquires all the conviction of a realistic portrait —a gruff but good-natured man, timid and violent, aggressive and resigned by turns. The identity between pictorial style and psychological insight could not be more explicit.

Understandably, the style of "the other side" involved a sacrifice of plastic energy. When, however, he resumed his crusade against vice and inveighed against woman, or rather against prostitution, he made a point of stressing plastic volume and relegated the style of "the other side" to the background or to details of secondary importance.

A group of nudes painted in 1906 and 1907 shows the sheer plastic power of this art carried to the extreme. It looks as if the painter deliberately dwelt on the massive bodies of these prostitutes in order to reveal their vulgarity, and relied on the shamelessness of their attitudes to drive home the full force of his moral condemnation. In the *Prostitute* of 1906 (Petit-Palais, Paris) the background of mingled lights and shadows and the black of hair and stockings are elements of great expressive power. In *Prostitute before a Mirror* of 1906 (Musée d'Art Moderne, Paris) the reflection in the glass is pictorially more effective than the face in the foreground, because it is streaked with heavy shadows more in keeping with the rest of the background. Here, as in the *Odalisque* of 1907 (Bangerter Collection, Montreux), we see how the picture space has not only been opened up, but is represented psychologically as well as physically, with the result that the representation is noticeably dematerialized. The gradual conquest of a style, in which the shamelessness of the nude is combined with a fully realized pictorial representation, affects both figure and background.

PROSTITUTES, 1910. BANGERTER COLLECTION, MONTREUX.

In this *Odalisque*, moreover, an interesting compositional principle is applied: the nude body is patterned with a linear rhythm that serves to equilibrate the plastic composition.

Let us turn to *Prostitutes* of 1910 (Bangerter Collection, Montreux). Effects of light and shade are here projected into the foreground, so as to emphasize the vehement handling of the nude bodies and to lessen their plastic density. There is no attenuation of his satirical aggressiveness, but the happy complexity of Rouault's style transforms it into pure art. Rouault had still another means of transcending the satirical, and that was to represent the female nude without castigating it, to represent it feelingly in all its natural beauty. Such is his *Bathers* (1907, Philippe Leclercq Collection, Hem), a watercolor all in calm tones of blue with scattered touches of red. Here is the work in which at last the female nude is sanctified, as it were, by its own beauty. These are Rouault's finest nudes—a foretaste of the glowing serenity of his later style.

Whenever the theme is unconcerned with the human figure, then, almost as a matter of course, the painterly style reappears and reasserts itself: for example, in *The Flood* (1910, Madame Simon Collection, Paris), where the vivid brushwork is completely identified with the vitality of nature, and above all in *Party at the Waterside* (1906, Madame Netter Collection, Paris), where the festive caperings of the brush seem to create new images at every turn.

The excellence of Rouault's work did not go long unnoticed. Roger Marx was the first critic to call attention to it, when he saw *The Child Jesus among the Doctors* at the Salon des Artistes Français in 1895. "I realize how much of it all is the result of schooling, how much Rouault owes to the museums, to the study of the Amsterdam master especially. All the same, his work has an unusual flavor which stamps it on our memory."[16]

In reviewing the 1896 Salon des Artistes Français Roger Marx had this to say: "Of Rouault's entries only one was accepted: *Christ mourned by the Holy Women*, the painting which raised such an outcry at the Ecole des Beaux-Arts when it appeared last year among the compositions competing for the Prix de Rome. Evidence of an assiduous study of the Old Masters is still visible, but a great talent reveals itself in the

THE FLOOD, 1910. MADAME SIMON COLLECTION, PARIS.

severe grouping of the figures and in the choice of this rich green tonality, spreading everywhere, which adds to the dramatic horror of the theme. Taking in the ten pictures at a single glance, one was struck by the contrast they offered, one could measure the full extent to which the teaching of Gustave Moreau towers above that of the other studios."[17] These comments indicate how much of a novelty this picture was considered to be at the time; what strikes us today as perfectly orthodox was regarded then as a revolt against academic tradition.

At the Salon d'Automne in 1903 and the following years Rouault showed pictures in a new vein, freed from academic ties and full of the breath of life—pictures that brought art back to reality. But the critics were bewildered by such a revolutionary change of heart. By 1904 Cézanne had ceased to be a public scandal; now it was Rouault's turn to scandalize.

Read, for example, the comments of Louis Vauxcelles in the *Gil Blas* of October 14, 1904. "Were it not that I know for a fact that Monsieur Rouault, curator of the Musée Moreau, is an artist of integrity, scrupulous and conscientious to a degree, and that I set a very high value on his powerful Hogarthian syntheses... I could hardly undertake to defend him against the jeering throng crowding around three or four of his 'dark pictures'. I know that his inspiration is sincere and painful. When he paints a prostitute, he does not take the cruel delight that Lautrec took in the odor of vice with which the creature reeks; it makes him suffer and weep. But oh! hapless painter of black, what a distressing mistake you have made! Are these Negresses in a tunnel? An illustration for a magazine entitled *The Invisible*? The eye sees nothing, nothing but caviar paste, boot polish and pitch... What kind of lighting does Rouault have in his studio? Does this misogynous dreamer wear smoked glasses to shut out nature and life, as he plunges into the depths of Hell?"

That Rouault had aroused great expectations is plain from the review published by Thiébault-Sisson in *Le Temps* on October 14, 1904. He was one of the most talked-about painters of the younger generation. "Not that he is lacking in charm or originality. Nothing could be more discreet and poetic than his twilight landscapes, or more appealing than his circus sketches. If only one could develop the same taste for his paintings. But we are repulsed by the impenetrability of their tones, inky black enlivened in places with purple accents, all of which seems, truth to tell, very much of a gamble."

In 1905, however, to the great dismay of the orthodox-minded, Thiébault-Sisson was more favorable. "Rouault is represented by a series of circus studies whose energy of accent and robustness of line go very far indeed. Rouault has the makings of a master and I for one am inclined to read into these things the prelude to a period of emancipation which will be marked by original creations and works of lasting value."

Even Charles Morice, the fastidious Symbolist and biographer of Gauguin, bore witness to the interest being taken in Rouault. In an article in the *Mercure de France* of December 1, 1905, he wrote: "Rouault undoubtedly has some surprises in store for us. May they come soon! All clear-sighted lovers of art hold him in the highest esteem and most of them are sorry to see him persevere in painful delineations of utter moral decay: *Prostitutes, Strolling Players, Clowns*. These titles confess to an obstinate pessimism which is not belied by the pictures themselves... Rouault is making his way through a night of tragic predicaments. Yet there seem to be faint lights ahead. *Twilight* says another title. Is it the twilight of morning or evening?"

Rouault's battle for recognition had begun and he pursued the path he had mapped out for himself, producing a great deal and steadily building up the style of which we have spoken. Two large one-man shows at the Galerie Druet in 1910 and 1911 confirmed the growing interest in his work, dedicated as it was to urgent social issues, and in spite of many reservations a wider comprehension of his efforts gradually developed.

In the preface to the catalogue of the 1910 exhibition Jacques Favelle wrote: "What we have here are not clever artifices intended to please, but naïve pictures of real life, made by a painstaking craftsman enamored of his tools and materials, who has simply set himself the task of reproducing as truthfully as possible the things that touch him emotionally. He speaks what he knows and feels, nothing more, nothing less, and neither to please nor to allure, nor to bring his initial emotion into line with any preconceived ideal. Every preliminary step, every correction, every line of investigation, is brought to bear on the means of expression. But always he moves straight ahead and his great virtue is frankness."

In the *Mercure de France* of January 16, 1912, Gustave Kahn paid tribute to the grace of his earlier religious pictures, and then added: "Now he turns a withering eye on his contemporaries. He does not find them to his liking. One can only suppose that, disheartened at seeing no trace in real life of the seraphic figures which he sought for at first, he now is venting his spleen on mankind at large by showing them in an unfavorable light. There is an undeniable driving power in his somber harmonies of purple glimpsed through darkness, and in his distortions of the human body, which he tears to pieces like a Juvenal of painting. The conversion of these fierce paintings into ceramics has yielded wholly new effects. To have been such an innovator is no mean achievement. Will this violent, satirical art be Rouault's last word? His is a resourceful mind; the old man, the emotional heart, the poet of yesteryears, may awaken within him, and it would be curious indeed to see the new manner that might be engendered in his work by a return to Eden, after this season in Hell."

Louis Vauxcelles, one of the first to take an interest in Rouault, endeavored several times to elucidate the secret of his painting, both by analysing his psychological referents and by defining his position in contemporary painting. Here is what he wrote in the *Gil Blas* of December 15, 1911: "This is the art of a visionary, a satirist who tears his victims apart, who suffers and moans. The depths of his backgrounds are lit up by magnificent tones. The tortured smiles of his figures freeze into

THREE JUDGES, 1913. MUSEUM OF MODERN ART, NEW YORK.

grimaces. For Rouault the humanity of modern times is a swarming mass of insects tormented with epileptic contortions. And having lashed out at his fellow men and distorted them beyond recognition, this bitter pessimist throws himself at the feet of the barbarous Christ which he has represented..."

In the *Carnet des Artistes* of June 15, 1917, Vauxcelles wrote: "Humanity as delineated by him is neither good-looking nor cheerful. Whose fault is this?... The secret of this harmony lies in his utter frankness, his steady pursuit of the absolute, his sovereign disregard of the adventitious, his dogged aspiration toward better things. Complex but singleminded, Rouault has always struggled on in the same direction. It was inevitable that he should in the end achieve this freedom, a freedom neither of pride nor of disorder, which we feel throughout his painting... The wheel has not yet turned full circle. But order will emerge from this apparent chaos."

The new order had already emerged in 1917. It consisted of a synthesis of planes and zones of color so contrived as to build up the picture independently of nature. Planes are located in the picture space with more precision than before, zones of color are correlated and harmonized with greater independence.

In 1913 Rouault painted four figures of wrestlers (formerly Henri Matisse Collection) which represent a landmark in his work because here, for the first time, he set out to paint nude figures in no way connected with social satire, caricature or any expressive purpose. His sole concern was with the organization of human figures within an undefined picture space.

Three Judges (Lewisohn Bequest, Museum of Modern Art, New York) also dates from 1913. It is not a very flattering picture, for Rouault had lost none of his antipathy for judges, though here it is implied rather than expressed; hence the pent-up energy of these exceptionally powerful figures.

THE OLD CLOWN, 1917. STAVROS NIARCHOS COLLECTION.

CRUCIFIXION, 1918.
COURTESY HENRY P. MCILHENNY, PHILADELPHIA.

The *Old Clown* of 1917 (formerly Edward G. Robinson Collection, now Niarchos Collection) and the *Sorrowful Clown* of about 1917 (Madame Simon Collection, Paris) are better suited than Judges to Rouault's new conception of independent form. His sympathy for clowns precluded any satirizing of them, so that now he could concentrate on the structuring of planes and the beauty of the colors, to the exclusion of expression. He was free to let his fancy roam, though in doing so was prompted not by a desire to break with traditional form (as he had done in the style of "the other side"), but by a determination to concentrate on form itself. The value of his abstract style lies in its identification with the compelling power of the image.

In 1918 Rouault painted the *Crucifixion* in the McIlhenny Collection, Philadelphia, which underlies all his later Crucifixions. Every onslaught against human cruelty, every emphasis on the pathetic, is ruled out; the result is an abstract composition of planes and colors which give form and spirit to a melancholy meditation on the Passion. The work as a whole has a grandeur and monumentality that lift the scene to a superhuman plane, such as only the art of the 13th century had attained.

Rouault had moved heaven and earth to overcome the limitations of the academic tradition. He had experienced for himself the religious revolution of Léon Bloy and had launched his own crusade against the vices and sham of Parisian society. Then he felt the necessity of transcending social satire, and thus created what I have called "the style of the other side"—which was in effect a caricatural style devoid of caricature. Lastly, he so far freed himself from the narrow bounds of daily life as to achieve the autonomy of the picture as a work of art on the strength of a style based on constructive planes. From 1903 to 1918 the essential themes and the formal principles of his painting were gradually established for good; all that remained was to develop them to the full.

MISERERE: WE THINK OURSELVES KINGS. PRINT, 1923.

BOOK ILLUSTRATIONS AND WRITINGS

A new force entered Rouault's life when Ambroise Vollard became his dealer. Acquiring the exclusive rights of his entire production, he commissioned Rouault to make an extensive series of book illustrations. As early as 1895 Vollard had published lithographs by Bonnard and others who were not professional engravers but painters. Little by little he realized his dream of establishing himself as a publisher of fine books handsomely produced and illustrated by the greatest contemporary artists. Owing to his insatiable desire for perfection, and also to the very large number of works which he commissioned, more in fact than he could handle, some of the outstanding masterpieces of modern engraving were still in his hands when he died in 1939 and were not published till after the Second World War. Among them was Rouault's *Miserere*. For many years, particularly during the 1920s, Rouault's activity as a printmaker was so engrossing that he found little time for painting. But all the while he broadened the cultural bases of his art, and also revealed himself as a writer of great originality.

His gifts as an illustrator were apparent even before 1918 in much of his painting; in the Prostitutes, for example. But after 1913, as we have noted, formal structure prevailed over illustration. So much so that when he turned to graphic work, he carried it out on the basis of a growing awareness of formal values and thus opened up new possibilities of expression —pictorial, technical, and broadly human.

In the years 1916-1917 and again from 1920 to 1927 Rouault devoted all his energies to a series of prints originally intended to illustrate two volumes, *Miserere* and *Guerre*, each with 50 large plates. But only 58 prints (etchings and aquatints) were finished; these were published in a single volume in 1948 under the title *Miserere* (Editions de l'Etoile Filante, Paris).

Miserere is a monumental achievement, sublime yet at the same time thoroughly popular in its appeal, and Rouault himself regarded it as a work of paramount importance in his output. The horrors of the 1914-1918 war weighed on his mind. He was no longer able to single out hateful features of contemporary society—it was all bad. The ravages of the war were too monstrous, and the artist took refuge in meditation and piety. His figures no longer had the realistic accents of an earlier phase, nor the resolute autonomy of structure characteristic of certain pictures painted after 1913. As Rouault explained in his preface to *Miserere*, he first executed drawings in India ink which, at Vollard's insistence, were transformed into paintings; from these, copper plates were made on which Rouault worked and reworked with different tools, through as many as twelve or fifteen successive states, in order to preserve the initial rhythm and draftsmanship. Hence the immediacy of his expression and its affirmative simplicity, which is emphasized by the colloquial tone of the captions: *The hard business of living, It would be so sweet to love, Far from the smile of Rheims, Dura lex sed lex.* Perhaps the only piece of caricature in *Miserere* is the king (*We think ourselves kings,* pl. 7), a souvenir perhaps of Ubu Roi. The sheer plastic power of certain plates is tremendous (pls. 12, 18, 35), while the picture of a harlot (pl. 14) spares our feelings and arouses no violent emotion, and the heaps of skulls around the Cross (pl. 28) assume a poetic remoteness. In *Sing matins, a new day is born* (pl. 29) we have perhaps the finest landscape that Rouault ever imagined, while in plates 9 and 23 he created a type of dramatic and religious landscape to which he reverted several times in his paintings.

It is important to remember that before being a great painter Rouault was a great draftsman, and that, in spite of a few chromatic innovations, it was not for his handling of color that he commanded attention before 1918. So that when he came

MISERERE: THE HARD BUSINESS OF LIVING. PRINT, 1922.

to dedicate himself to the graphic work of *Miserere* Rouault rediscovered the medium of expression most congenial to him.

Between 1916 and 1928 Rouault worked on the 22 etchings and aquatints and 104 designs for wood engravings which went to illustrate *Les Réincarnations du Père Ubu* (published in 1932), a book written by Ambroise Vollard as a sequel to Alfred Jarry's *Ubu Roi*. Less dramatic and more whimsical than *Miserere*, the subject matter did not take so firm a grip of the artist's mind. In such plates as *Negro Porter* and *Negro with Upraised Arms* he surrendered to the impulses of his fancy. *Negro beside a Tree* is a gracious idyll, with a composition of lilting rhythms. Then there is the fantastic beast in mid-air, a monstrous assemblage of incongruous forms, absolutely grotesque.

The illustrations of Baudelaire's *Les Fleurs du Mal* promised to be a masterpiece of macabre art, but Rouault only finished a few of the plates. Two of them, executed in 1926 and 1927, form a kind of *danse macabre* and hauntingly express the sense of total despair conveyed by the idea of death.

In addition to this work, commissioned by Vollard, Rouault executed a whole series of lithographs for the French publisher E. Frapier: those of *Maîtres et Petits Maîtres* and several magnificent portraits illustrating his *Souvenirs Intimes* (published in 1926), those for example of Baudelaire, Moreau, Verlaine and the artist himself. In 1929 he published a series of six lithographs entitled *Petite Banlieue* (Editions des Quatre Chemins), and then six lithographs and fifty drawings for *Paysages Légendaires* (Editions Porteret) in which he indulged in idyllic fantasies rudely shaken, however, by the pulsating abundance of life from which they spring. Here a new accent is discernible: a penchant for decorative composition.

After 1930 Rouault turned to color etchings and aquatints. His renewed interest in painting during the thirties led him to seek after similar chromatic effects in etching, and indeed

MISERERE: SING MATINS, A NEW DAY IS BORN. PRINT, 1922.

MISERERE: HE THAT BELIEVETH IN ME, THOUGH HE WERE DEAD, YET SHALL
HE LIVE. PRINT, 1923.

MISERERE: DEAD MEN, ARISE! PRINT, 1923.

BAUDELAIRE, LES FLEURS DU MAL: BRIDE AND GROOM. LITHOGRAPH, 1926.

he brought them off in this medium quite as proficiently as in his paintings. These works were very favorably received by the public, but it is sometimes maintained that they lack the emotional driving force of the earlier plates in black and white, and that therefore they represent a decline. I cannot share this view. Admittedly Rouault's color etchings do not convey the same degree of moral, social and religious passion as the black and white work. But in them appears a new passion, in harmony with the paintings produced after 1930: a passion for new pictorial form, equilibrated and contrasted, infused with unprecedented power and dignity. The direction of Rouault's taste had changed, but we must take care not to confuse a change of direction with progress or decline.

Rouault's color etchings and aquatints were commissioned by Vollard to illustrate *Le Cirque de l'Etoile Filante*, published in 1938 with a text by Rouault himself (17 color etchings and aquatints and 82 black-and-white wood engravings), and *Passion*, published in 1938 with a text by André Suarès (17 color etchings and aquatints and 82 black-and-white wood engravings). In 1934-1935 he made some color etchings for another book by André Suarès, *Le Cirque*, as yet unpublished.

During the thirties Rouault also executed three large color etchings and four large lithographs, all commissioned by Vollard. In 1939 he made a color etching for the de luxe edition of my first monograph on him and his work (New York, 1940).

Rouault's graphic work very quickly achieved an international success, thus anticipating the success of his painting. In 1938 the Museum of Modern Art in New York sponsored an exhibition of his prints, with a catalogue by Monroe Wheeler. The comprehensive exhibition of his work as a whole, at the same museum, was not held till 1945. The prints commissioned by Vollard have been carefully catalogued by Una E. Johnson in her *Ambroise Vollard Editeur* (New York, 1944)

SOUVENIRS INTIMES: PORTRAIT OF BAUDELAIRE. LITHOGRAPH, 1926.

SOUVENIRS INTIMES: PORTRAIT OF VERLAINE. LITHOGRAPH, 1926.

Absorbed as he was in the reading and illustrating of books, Rouault was moved to commit his own thoughts and feelings to writing, and thus, both in poems and critical articles, he made his own contribution to an intelligent understanding of his work and of the spiritual climate of present-day art in general. Rouault published some critical notes on Cézanne, Carrière and Rodin as early as 1910 in the *Mercure de France*. His most important essays in criticism are to be found in *Souvenirs Intimes* (1926), but he also published articles of more general interest in *Les Cahiers du Mois* (1925), *L'Amour de l'Art* (1927), *Chroniques du Jour* (1931), *Cahiers d'Art* (1935), *Revue de l'Art Ancien et Moderne* (1936), *Beaux-Arts* (1936), *Renaissance* (1937), *Verve* (1939) and *Le Point* (1943).

Only a small part of Rouault's poetical works has been published, notably in *Paysages Légendaires* (1929), *Le Cirque de l'Etoile Filante* (1938) and *Stella Vespertina* (1947). Poems by Rouault have also appeared in *Les Soirées de Paris* (1914), *L'Amour de l'Art* (1925), *Bulletin de la Vie Artistique* (1925) and *Verve* (1939 and 1940).

His most important work, however, in the field of poetry is *Soliloques*, published in Switzerland in 1944 (Ides et Calendes, Neuchâtel). This is an anthology of Rouault's poetry, selected by Claude Roulet from 1200 manuscript sheets of poems written during the First World War and from 250 more written between 1940 and 1944. All were composed in wartime, during periods of enforced idleness, when he found it impossible to paint and so was moved to express himself in words.

Claude Roulet prefaced the book with a sensitive analysis of Rouault's style of writing, a few passages of which it may be worth while quoting here.

"Rouault's style follows the spoken language of the people. Like the vernacular, it is racy, natural, direct, colorful. Though it is simple, by which I mean cursory, clear, colloquial, it is by no means easy to describe. The reason is that this style is original, and that, among all the forms of originality, it is the vivid expression of a complex nature. Whether he takes his vocabulary from one idiom or another of Paris, from the idiom of the peasant, the sailor, the soldier, he undergoes a spontaneous metamorphosis; there is a change of tone, of line, of face, and one local color is substituted for another. He delicately evokes the subtlest features which go to make up the atmosphere and the natural movement of life...

"When his style follows the idiom of the street, his sentences consist of the ready-made phrases also used by flower girls, by harlots, by gossiping housewives. There are many texts of this kind. From a literary point of view, these are not the best. While they make good reading in manuscript, they lose something when printed. They are phrased in brisk, direct, idiomatic terms, a zestful, vivid style. The running narrative, taken straight from the life, smacks of vaudeville: comic without being vulgar, glib, swift-moving and colorful, it never bores you."[18]

The same applies to the style of his painting—the same and something more besides, because of course Rouault was committed to painting heart and soul, while literature after all was only a side line with him. Painting was his whole life; it was his Inferno and his Paradiso, while his writings were a kind of limbo where he could relieve his spirits of excess anguish and excess joy, and measure his strength with that of the people around him.

GROTESQUE, 1927. HADORN COLLECTION, BERN.

SERENITY REGAINED

THE twelve years from 1918 to 1930 were for Rouault a period of anxiety, of extra-pictorial ventures, and there was a slackening of his activity as a painter. It is not always realized that this pause was also marked by a ripening of Rouault's painterly faculties, and that by devoting himself to book illustration he discovered for himself everything that differentiates the illustrator from the painter. Nor is it always realized how steadily he progressed, now visibly, now imperceptibly, amassing a wealth of new experience. He painted much less during those years than he ever had before. But when about 1928 he resumed painting, it became apparent that new pictorial powers had developed within him, unbeknown even to Rouault himself. These were a revelation for everyone when he exhibited at the Petit-Palais in Paris in 1937.

The positive element of these new powers was tenacity —the tenacity of the craftsman. Rouault's reluctance to finish a picture and part with it is almost proverbial. He would tackle it anew, again and again, twenty or thirty times. He would bungle it, then recreate it in a new and finer form. Again he would tinker with it and spoil it, then somehow resurrect it and give it eternal life. In the end he grudgingly signed it and watched it leave his studio with the greatest misgivings. He made no secret of his hostility to the photographers who came to "snap" an early state of a painting for prospective buyers. Once he had gone back to work and altered the picture, he insisted on having the photographic plate destroyed.

When asked what his intentions were as he superimposed one color on another, Rouault used to reply that he was seeking a richer, more accurate tone, and a more opulent color scheme. The more intense and varied the colors, the more difficult it was to obtain that color scheme. But underlying this pursuit of the right tone was a spiritual process far wider in scope. It was a check, a disciplinary measure, unknown in art before Impressionism, and this, in 1874, Cézanne had laid down as a law in the following terms: "I work at a picture again and again, but not to attain the finish that excites the admiration of fools... I only seek to complete the picture for the sake of making it a truer, more skillful piece of work." In other words, to "complete" a picture is not to give it the sleek finish of 19th-century academic art, but to achieve that disciplined state of unfinish which constitutes one of the greatest conquests of modern taste, and which is the check, the discipline imposed on art by Rouault. His paintings from about 1930 on exemplify the unique and sovereign success with which he arrived at this result.

He now reworked many older paintings and sketches until he was satisfied that they were *alive*. Figures and objects seemed lifeless to him until he had steeped them in colors full of transparencies, reflections, highlights. The color scheme seemed drab to him until the superimposed layers of paints came to evoke all the colors of the rainbow, in a strange phantasmagoria. His art has always led critics to speak of stained glass, of enamels, of precious stones. The explanation is that his color schemes are gemlike because they consist of a thousand different hues; their harmony is rich and gorgeous because it embraces all harmonies. His color combinations are often so unerring, the effect is so rich and intricate, that the spectator is overwhelmed, he is wonderstruck and baffled at the same time, because he finds himself at a loss to explain how and why these numberless colors are made to fuse into a *single* color.

This method of work, with its continual reversals of direction, its continual recastings and revisions, always leading him to add rather than delete, to combine more and more colors— this method had the effect of carrying Rouault farther and farther from his initial religious and social preoccupations.

Perhaps, in its earlier state, the picture had been scathing or satirical; nothing of this remained in the finished painting. Too many layers of paint had gone on to the canvas, too much work had been expended in pursuit of the new form, which in the end wholly absorbed his original intentions. Rouault's indictment of evil and injustice, his distortions and grotesque effects, all were contained and implied in the finished work; they were the life, the content of his new art. But form comprised and overruled them now, it was no longer dependent on them.

CIRCUS TRIO, C. 1924. PHILLIPS COLLECTION, WASHINGTON.

NUDE, AFTER 1930. COURTESY OF A. A. JUVILER, NEW YORK.

The form of the grotesque and satirical was there, without the grotesque and satirical themselves. It was a triumph of color such as had never been seen before, a triumph of fluid form replete with delicate nuances, and marked, above all, by a serenity and freedom born of the fully conscious exercise of untrammeled self-expression.

The self-portrait known as *The Prentice Craftsman* (Musée d'Art Moderne, Paris) must have been painted about 1925, since it corresponds to the lithographed *Self-Portrait* in his *Souvenirs Intimes* (1926). The painting is remarkable for its beauty and perfection of form. The *Circus Trio* of about 1924 (Phillips Collection, Washington) contains new elements of synthesis but is still grotesque in spirit. The same is true of the *Grotesque* of 1927 (Hadorn Collection, Bern), a masterpiece of formal liberty and color steeped in light.

The *Nude* in the Juviler Collection, New York, exemplifies the perfectly accomplished style achieved by Rouault after 1930. Compared with a work of 1918, like the McIlhenny *Crucifixion*, the novelty of this *Nude* is obvious: color is no longer subordinate to a structural basis, no longer fitted into the linear design; on the contrary, contours are born together with color, which is to say that color constitutes the very structure of form. So now for the first time Rouault's painting joins up with medieval stained glass, and acquires the phosphorescent colors characteristic of it. The effect is one of painterly volume rather than plastic relief, and stems entirely from color: deep-toned, intense, richly varied colors, all in shimmering transparencies, which reveal form just as it comes to life, colors which do not burst upon us but float slowly to the surface. The essence of such painting as this is the serene dignity it lends to the human figure. Rouault was nearing sixty, he had been relieved of material worries, he was entirely wrapped up in his art: into it he poured his own goodness of heart, his regrets, his piety,

CEMETERY, 1930. PASTEL. PHILIPPE LECLERCQ COLLECTION, HEM.

the purified, serenely exalted faith of old age. Satirical effects have vanished, yet they are always implied beneath the surface and they remain a vital element. Thus it may fairly be said that this new art embodied the form of the grotesque and satirical without the grotesque and satirical themselves.

By its very nature this type of painting was well suited to the rendering of landscape and in fact several of Rouault's landscapes are datable to the thirties: *Landscape beside the Sea* (Museum of Modern Art, New York), *Cemetery* (Philippe Leclercq Collection, Hem), *Landscape* (Charles Im Obersteg Collection, Geneva). These have highly synthetic forms whose sole function is to provide support for the colors, which are generally so intense as to convey the glow, the vitality, with which, in Rouault's eyes at least, everything in nature is saturated. The vitality and vibrancy he had given his graphic work is here rendered in color to even greater effect, broad and cosmic in its sweep.

The decade of the thirties was rich in masterpieces. Although, as noted, Rouault merely elaborated on themes and pictures which he had sketched out before 1916, he transformed them so radically as to make them look like new inventions and discoveries. The pictorial style he had created before 1930 made it necessary for him to transform every line into a zone

LANDSCAPE, 1930-1939. CHARLES IM OBERSTEG COLLECTION, GENEVA.

THE LAST ROMANTIC, 1937.
DR. AND MRS. HARRY BAKWIN, NEW YORK.

THE OLD KING, 1937.
COURTESY OF CARNEGIE INSTITUTE, PITTSBURGH.

89

of color, to enrich that color to an almost fabulous degree, and then to build up not only color-forms but color-motifs.

Take, for example, *The Old King* (Carnegie Institute, Pittsburgh). It originally dates from 1916, but that was only a beginning. In its final form—for it was not finished till 1937, twenty years after the initial version—it is one of Rouault's greatest color creations. Now it is precisely its phosphorescent color, almost like stained glass enclosed in a painting, that gives the picture of the Old King not only its formal structure, but also its regal dignity, its noble melancholy. Rouault's palette is here endowed with a new quality: phosphorescence. By superimposing layer upon layer of paint, by his tireless pursuit of what he called "the true tone," Rouault elicited something magical from the canvas: light, instead of impinging on it, seems to emanate from the picture itself. So that even when tones are dark, they glow with a light from within. This is what makes his handling of color unique; with Rouault we turn a page in the history of art and enter on a new era of color in painting. Rembrandt, Daumier, Cézanne, the great worshippers of light who pursued it into the depths of shadows, would certainly acknowledge, could they be ushered into the presence of this art, that the smoldering phosphorescence of Rouault's colors is something new.

The Last Romantic (Dr. Harry Bakwin Collection, New York) is an equally powerful work. This is the portrait of a dandy who, with his studied elegance of dress, is almost as much out of place in the modern world as the Old King. But now there are even bolder contrasts of tone, and these alone build up the figure. The effigy of a medieval king has given place to an effigy of the 18th century. In *The Last Romantic* a hint of satire floats to the surface and gives a rugged virility to the face, but it is attenuated by the elegance of the costume and the beauty of the colors, whose vitality is imbued with an exceptional intensity.

THE DWARF, 1937. COURTESY OF THE ART INSTITUTE OF CHICAGO.

HEAD OF A WOMAN, 1939. PRIVATE COLLECTION, ROME.

POLYCARP, 1937-1938. COLLECTION OF FRAU HAFTER-KOTTMANN, SOLOTHURN.

WOUNDED CLOWN, C. 1933. PRIVATE COLLECTION, PARIS.

94

Now as always Rouault found inspiration in clowns. Two pictures painted round about 1937 show only the head, with the merest hint of shoulders and costume: *Benito* (formerly Pierre Berès Collection) and *The Dwarf* (Art Institute of Chicago). These large heads seen in close-up, with their features chiseled out of a uniform background, produce an effect of plastic violence. They stand out saliently from the canvas, but it is an effect of psychological projection rather than actual physical relief. These figures, like *The Old King*, initiate us into the secret of Rouault's color. *Benito* stands out against a blue background, with orange-pink flesh tints, a grey-green cap and patches of yellow on the shoulders. The painter succeeded in obtaining phosphorescent effects with streaks of chrome yellow over black and blue. Seen against the dark background, the flesh tints glow like meteors in the night. The artist no doubt began two such pictures as *Benito* and *The Dwarf* in a spirit of burlesque or satire; but this mood succumbed, in the final execution, to the artistic impulse, and the aggressiveness and driving force of the initial inspiration were in the end concentrated on the formal creation.

Many heads and busts, often brilliantly inventive works, date from the thirties. *Head of a Woman* (1939, Private Collection, Rome) is remarkable for an animated rhythm of lights and shadows and intense colors; the face is one of arresting beauty in spite of the fact that the features are more abstract than real. More traditional in form is the fine head of *Polycarp* (1937-1938, Collection of Frau Hafter-Kottmann, Solothurn, Switzerland), also remarkable for its fabulous wealth of color effects.

Ever since the early years of revolt, Rouault had focused his attention on figures rather than composition; even when some elaboration of the latter had been required in order to situate a figure group, it was not to the composition that the picture owed its esthetic value. But in the lucid serenity of later years, when his interest had finally come to center on form and color, it was only natural for him to give more thought to problems of composition.

Wounded Clown (c. 1933, Private Collection, Paris) is a large canvas, of a size unusual for Rouault. On the left we see the painter himself, dressed as a clown, condoling with his wounded companion. The two clowns in the foreground bend to a rhythm of form and attitude which gives an abstract value to the scene. Posed along a diagonal in such a way as to indicate spatial recession, the three figures are balanced by the moon and clouds above, whose forms and volumes constitute a striking fragment in themselves. Rouault made no secret here of his decorative intentions, and this composition has actually served as the cartoon for a tapestry.

During the thirties, needless to say, Rouault continued to treat religious themes, the Crucifixion first of all, of which he made several versions. One of the finest, datable to 1939, was still in the artist's possession at his death. A comparison with the McIlhenny *Crucifixion* of 1918 shows some notable differences. To build up his figures and composition in 1939 he no longer relied on the heavily outlined zones of color which he used in 1918. Everything now is stark and synthetic, richer in plastic energy, with amplified effects of spatial depth, in a word more monumental. Dramatic expression no longer stems from faces and gestures, but solely from a harmony of forms. In 1918 the figures alone were involved in the action; in 1939 they melt into an all-pervading poetic atmosphere of melancholy contemplation created by spiritualized colors. Here the cursive linework of *Miserere* has been developed to its full expressive capacity, yielding a result so alien to reality, so remote from daily life, so elevated and transcendent, that we should have to go back to the 13th century, so dear to Léon Bloy, and to the painting of Cimabue to find a line equally

CRUCIFIXION, 1939. OWNED BY THE ARTIST'S FAMILY.

OUR JOAN, 1940-1948.
PRIVATE COLLECTION, PARIS.

imbued with spirituality. The *Head of Christ* (Cleveland Museum of Art), painted about 1937-1938, again reveals the extent to which Rouault was capable of bringing out the profoundest spiritual implications of a religious image.

Our Joan (Private Collection, Paris) was painted between 1940 and 1948; it was a theme to which he reverted several times. The powerful currents of his faith and patriotism met and mingled in Rouault's lifelong veneration of Joan of Arc. On such a

CHRIST ON THE LAKE OF TIBERIAS, 1939.
PRIVATE COLLECTION, ROME.

END OF AUTUMN, NO. 3, 1948-1952.
PRIVATE COLLECTION, PARIS.

HEAD OF CHRIST, 1937-1938.
THE CLEVELAND MUSEUM OF ART, GIFT OF HANNA FUND.

TWILIGHT (CHRIST AND DISCIPLES), 1937-1938.
PHILIPPE LECLERCQ COLLECTION, HEM.

theme it is not surprising to find him, like an inspired mystic, rising to new heights of expression, couched in magnificent phosphorescent colors. The monumentality of the heroine and her charger is effectively magnified by contrast with a thin strip of landscape visible in the distance. Here again it must be admitted that, while the picture has all the complexity and subtlety of modern art at its best, its spirit is that of an equestrian monument of the Quattrocento rather than a work of 1940.

SUNSET, 1937-1938. COLLECTION OF MRS. ALDUS C. HIGGINS. ON LOAN AT THE WORCESTER ART MUSEUM.

THE FLIGHT INTO EGYPT, 1940-1948.
PRIVATE COLLECTION, PARIS.

END OF AUTUMN, NO. 4, 1948-1952.
COLLECTION OF MR. AND MRS. PAUL H. SAMPLINER, NEW YORK.

This period of regained serenity might also be described as a period of concentration on pictorial technique rather than on imagery. So it was only natural for Rouault's interest in landscape (already noted in his work of the twenties) to continue unabated and even increase. He probably found, as others had before him, that landscape is less engrossing than the human figure and thus allows greater licence to the creative imagination.

After 1932 he invented a new type of landscape, which had only been hinted at in his earlier work. These new landscapes are visions of the East, seen in the light of the setting sun and peopled with figures amongst whom we often discern that of Christ. They are variations on the same theme: under the glowing sky of Palestine, in an indistinct setting, the shadow of death and of night falls over the tragedy of Christ. They might be described as Rouault's sacred landscapes.

Such is *Sunset* (Worcester Art Museum), for example. Figures and objects are roughly sketched in, dimly visible through a swirling harmony of gorgeous colors. Figures make no gestures: they are presented, not represented, with the result that the whole dramatic effect of the work springs from the colors and the desolation of the scene. That desolation recurs in all Rouault's landscapes. For him, apparently, the earth was a wasteland; even the houses are dismal; their occupants wander among them as among so many ruins. Christ and a few paupers represent humanity amid this desolation. Life and light are only to be sought above, in the heavens. This is an apocalyptic vision of nature, its bleakness redeemed only by the thirst for color and light, by the sustaining aspiration toward a Kingdom not of this world. Dedicated to the setting sun, these landscapes contain some of Rouault's loveliest visions of color.

Christ on the Lake of Tiberias (Private Collection, Rome), for example, is charged with a tremendous chromatic intensity: the two yellows of sky and lake absorb light and leave the earth shrouded in a penumbra of deeper tones. A more constructive work, *End of Autumn, No. 4* (Paul H. Sampliner Collection, New York) is built up around the mass of the hill, crowned with its inevitable minaret.

After 1940 Rouault's style steadily evolved in the direction of a greater concentration on pictorial effects and a more rigorous stripping away of non-essentials. Between 1940 and

1948, working predominantly in blues, he greatly enriched his colors, which took on a new depth and density. After 1948 various shades of green, yellow and red prevailed over blue, and these combined in new plays of shimmering color.

The Flight into Egypt (1940-1948, Private Collection, Paris) is a religious scene in a landscape setting. We get the impression, however, that the landscape itself took the artist's fancy and held it, for the religious mood derives mainly from the light kindled by the color patches that serve to block out forms.

Autumn (Vatican Museum) has none of the spatial complications of an earlier picture of the same name, anterior to 1937. The trees now have thinned out and spatial depth, instead of being rendered with optical illusionism, is merely suggested psychologically. The same is true of *Winter* (formerly Louis Carré Collection, Paris). Although the receding row of houses suggests space, it seems to do so fortuitously, without the artist's intervention; intent as he was on subordinating the physical to the spiritual, Rouault was impelled to revert to a primitive conception of space. In *End of Autumn, No. 3* (Private Collection, Paris) the perspective is deliberately distorted in order to emphasize the imposing spiritual eminence of the distant temple. Here again it was the repudiation of "correct" spatial recession that set his imagery free.

Both before and after 1940 Rouault painted many flower pieces. These were the best possible pretext for showing off a glittering array of colors, displayed for their own sake with no concern for representational details. As a rule his bouquets are composed of imaginary flowers, pure creations of art, usually with a decorative frame painted round them. *Decorative Flowers* (Private Collection, Paris) is an excellent example.

Pierrot too continued to inspire the artist, and in *The Aristocrat Pierrot* (Philippe Leclercq Collection, Hem) we have one of his masterpieces. With easy grace the isolated figure stands

THE ARISTOCRAT PIERROT, 1942.
PHILIPPE LECLERCQ COLLECTION, HEM.

out against a landscape background, like the sprite of a fairy tale or a heraldic device designed to set off the arabesque. Blue-green is contrasted with blue and orange, and orange reflections flicker across the face—calm, full-toned colors in exquisite harmonies. *The Wise Pierrot* (Alex Hillman Collection, New York) is an equally graceful figure, more realistically posed in a more fully delineated setting. Both of these Pierrots date to the 1940s. Such works as *Seraphine*, another *Pierrot* and an *Ecce Homo* (all in private collections, Paris), on the other hand, show a progressive absorption of the figure into the surrounding color, which glows with increasing incandescence, with a shimmering wealth of tones carried to the extreme limits of the painter's medium.

Fame came slowly to Rouault. His gifts were noticed and written about as early as 1895, and though in the years preceding the First World War he received a certain amount of recognition, many critics remained hostile to his work. After 1918, with his entire production controlled by Vollard and his own time and energies almost entirely devoted to graphic work, Rouault gradually found himself cut off from the art world of Paris.

Still, several one-man exhibitions of his work took place: in 1920 at the Galerie La Licorne; in 1922 at the Galerie Barbazanges; and, in 1924, at the Galerie Druet, a large retrospective grouping eighty-eight paintings and eight ceramics. But little notice was taken of them, and in *L'Amour de l'Art* of December 1923 we find André Lhote writing: "No more is said about Rouault. He holds no more exhibitions, and is there anyone who can boast of having met him at a party or a *vernissage*?" Rouault had not been forgotten by the critics, but in discussing him now they had nothing but his pre-war work to go on. In 1920 Gustave Coquiot devoted a chapter to him in his book *Les Indépendants*; Michel Puy wrote the first monograph

THE WISE PIERROT, 1940-1948.
COLLECTION OF MR. AND MRS. ALEX L. HILLMAN, NEW YORK.

DECORATIVE FLOWERS, 1948-1952.
PRIVATE COLLECTION, PARIS.

ECCE HOMO, 1952.
PRIVATE COLLECTION, PARIS.

on him in 1921 in the series *Les Peintres français nouveaux*, published by the *Nouvelle Revue Française*; Jacques Maritain wrote an article on him in *La Revue Universelle* of May 15, 1924; and Georges Charensol published a new monograph in 1926, the most complete study up to that time, illustrated with forty plates, of which only three or four reproduced post-war paintings—which shows how difficult it was even for the most zealous to penetrate the veil that hung over his recent work.

No change in this situation was produced by the small exhibitions at the Galerie des Quatre Chemins in 1926, 1929 and 1931, or at the Galerie Bing in 1927; nor by the commission from Diaghilev to paint the sets for Prokofiev's *Prodigal Son* (1929); nor by the new stirrings of interest in the artist outside France in 1930 with the exhibitions at the Brummer Gallery in New York, the Arts Club of Chicago, the St. George's Gallery in London, the Neumann Gallery in Munich, or in 1931 at the Galerie Schwarzenberg in Brussels.

In 1917 the French Government had purchased Rouault's first painting, *The Child Jesus among the Doctors* (Musée d'Unterlinden, Colmar)—a work dating from 1894! But in 1930, when it was officially proposed to acquire a painting by Rouault for the Musée du Luxembourg in Paris, the State refused. Not until 1933 did it accept one of his works, and this was a donation made by Mrs. Chester Dale.

Meanwhile several critics had been trying to draw the public's attention to him. In 1928 the *Cahiers d'Art* published an issue containing several articles on Rouault, among them an excellent study by Georges Chabot. From 1930 dates the small book by Raymond Cogniat in the series *Les Artistes Nouveaux*, and from 1931 the essay by Marcel Arland in the July issue of the *Nouvelle Revue Française*. In 1933 came the studies of Paul Fierens (in *L'Amour de l'Art*, June) and Sam A. Lewisohn (in *Parnassus*, November). In 1936 R. Ito published a Rouault

SERAPHINE, 1948-1952.
PRIVATE COLLECTION, PARIS.

BITTER SWEET, 1948-1952.
PRIVATE COLLECTION, PARIS.

album at Tokyo in which, for the first time, we find reproductions of various post-war works. At Neuchâtel (Switzerland) in 1937 Claude Roulet published some notes on Rouault's art and several texts by the artist himself. These books and articles gradually made Rouault better known, but his fame grew very slowly, almost stealthily.

The situation changed radically in 1937 when a whole room was devoted to Rouault at the exhibition "Les Maîtres de l'Art Indépendant," held at the Petit-Palais in conjunction with the Paris World's Fair. Rouault himself selected and arranged the pictures, which provided an excellent cross-section of his output since 1918. Nothing so comprehensive had been seen since the 1924 retrospective at Druet's, and even that exhibition had consisted mainly of more or less well-known works. The 1937 exhibition, on the other hand, revealed his mature post-war style for the first time, and once in the presence of these paintings, visitors found it hard to tear themselves away. It was a triumph for Rouault, and by general consent he took his rightful place among the great masters of modern art. There were still a few detractors to contend with, but their following soon melted away. In the course of a friendly discussion about this time with Louis Vauxcelles—who had discerned Rouault's genius in 1905—he asked me if it was true that I was preparing a book on Rouault. When I told him that it was quite true, he replied, re-echoing a phrase of Renoir's: *"Ce sera le livre d'un fou sur un fou."* No one, myself least of all, anticipated the success which the book was to have.

Tidings of the 1937 exhibition at the Petit-Palais were not slow to reach America. In November of the same year the Pierre Matisse Gallery in New York organized a large Rouault exhibition. In 1938 the Museum of Modern Art in New York held its memorable exhibition of Rouault's prints. The first edition of my book on Rouault was published in New York by

PIERROT, 1948-1952. PRIVATE COLLECTION, PARIS.

E. Weyhe in 1940. In the same year three great American museums jointly sponsored a Rouault retrospective: the Institute of Modern Art in Boston, the Phillips Memorial Gallery in Washington, and the San Francisco Museum of Art. Exhibitions were held in New York at the Bignou Gallery in 1940 and at the Marie Harriman Gallery in 1941. In 1945 came the large Rouault retrospective at the Museum of Modern Art, New York. In 1946 the Tate Gallery in London showed a selection of paintings and etchings, while the Galerie Drouin in Paris held an exhibition of religious art centering on Rouault's work. His latest paintings were shown in 1947 at the Pierre Matisse Gallery, New York, and the Galerie des Garets, Paris.

Rouault was represented at the Venice Biennale of 1948 by twenty-six paintings and sixteen engravings, while the Kunsthaus in Zurich sponsored the largest exhibition so far devoted to the artist: the catalogue listed 263 items. Rouault retrospectives were held in 1952 at the Palais des Beaux-Arts in Brussels, the Stedelijk Museum in Amsterdam, and the Musée d'Art Moderne in Paris; in 1953 at the Cleveland Museum of Art, the County Museum of Los Angeles, and the Museum of Modern Art, New York; in 1954 at the Galleria d'Arte Moderna in Milan, and in 1956 at the Musée Toulouse-Lautrec in Albi. Rouault's work has thus become familiar to art lovers of the whole world.

Many exhibitions, then, have been held since 1940, and the literature on Rouault has increased accordingly. Two monographs, however, deserve special mention: those of Marcel Brion (1950) and Bernard Dorival (1956). The biographical material contained in the latter was endorsed by the artist himself and I acknowledge my indebtedness to it here.

A few other recent events are worth recording. For years, in spite of the efforts undertaken on his behalf by the French Dominicans, the Catholic Church gave no official recognition to the religious art practised by Rouault. In 1945, however, Canon Devemy and Father Couturier commissioned him to design five stained-glass windows for the church of Assy (Haute-Savoie); these were executed by Hébert Stevens and Paul Bony. It was not until 1953 that the pope officially paid honor to Rouault.

In 1947 the artist brought a lawsuit against the heirs of Ambroise Vollard for the recovery of nearly 800 unfinished, unsigned paintings which had been in Vollard's possession at the time of his death in 1939. Rouault won his suit and the pictures were returned to him. Before witnesses, on November 5, 1948, he burned 315 of them, which he felt he would never be able to finish.

Rouault designed several tapestry cartoons which were executed by Madame Marie Cuttoli in the early thirties. He also designed some enamels which were executed in 1949 in the monastic workshops of the Abbey of Liguré (Vienne). In 1951, for his 80th birthday, a celebration was held in his honor at the Palais de Chaillot in Paris and Abbé Morel gave the first showing of his film on Rouault's *Miserere*.

He went on working in solitude to the very end, and died on February 13, 1958, at the age of 86.

The art of Georges Rouault, like much of the art of our time, is a surmounting of elements in contrast. In his youth, as we have seen, he rebelled against the academic tradition in which he had done such fine work—so fine that there was some danger of his remaining entangled in the academic routine. All the more violent, therefore, was the revolt that freed him from it. The difficulties of that liberation were rendered doubly acute by his deep-seated religious convictions. All modern art has been born and bred in a non-religious climate, in keeping with modern thought and modern culture in general. For a painter to produce "modern art" on religious themes, with a religious inspiration, seemed like a contradiction in terms. When at the end of the 19th century Léon Bloy crusaded for a revival of religious life, he met with a deep response in many an awakened conscience; but the effect lasted no more than a generation. Yet today, fifty-five years after Rouault's revolt, his art has lost none of its appeal and actuality, even though it increasingly isolated the painter himself.

With their harmonies of timbre rather than tone, Rouault's color schemes bring to mind the great stained-glass windows of the 13th century, while his conception of form as exemplified in his Crucifixions recalls Cimabue. His spiritual affinities, then, are not with his contemporaries, like Picasso, or his classmate Matisse, but with the great religious painters of the 13th century.

This being so, it seems paradoxical that Rouault should have taken to modern painting. But it is only a seeming paradox when we remember the key role that successive revolts have played in modern art. Indeed, to carry the parallel even further, let it be remembered that modern political life begins with the French Revolution, and our intellectual life with the Romantic revolution. Modern philosophical thought has been conditioned by a whole series of ideological upheavals, often in combination with each other; the same is true of music and the plastic arts.

It was his revolt that saved Rouault from academicism and made him a modern artist—the imperative need he felt to express his religious convictions not in pictures of angels, but in an indictment of vice and evil; and to rediscover the truths of Christianity not in principles of faith, but in the lives of clowns and unfortunates. So wholeheartedly sincere was his revolt that it enabled him to express a 13th-century ideal in an art of the present day.

So momentous a change in his spiritual outlook could not take place without equally momentous changes in his conception of form. Rouault had to fight on several fronts. First he broke free of academic tradition; by doing so he rejected an art he knew by rote and reverted to the status of a primitive—which did not of course prevent him from applying all the knowledge and skill he had acquired. He thereupon invented what I have called "the style of the other side," in which lines no longer coincide with contours, and shadows prevail over light. From 1903 to the present day, pictorial form has undergone many transformations, chiefly under the influence of Cubism and abstract art. But Rouault always remained impervious to their influence, almost as if he were living on another planet. He too of course achieved a synthesis, a hieratic simplicity, a breaking down of forms, which have nothing in common with realism —which led him, on the contrary, to a subjective expression of the transcendental. But his way of attaining that end differed fundamentally from that of his contemporaries, and though he may rightfully be called a French expressionist, it goes without saying that he had nothing in common with his German contemporaries who also felt impelled to practise Expressionism.

To reconcile heaven and earth, past and present, realism and abstraction, the image and the style of the other side, tonal intensity and color harmony—such was the work of a man of adamantine moral integrity and an artist of genius whose stature will continue to increase with the passing of time.

TEXT REFERENCES
BIBLIOGRAPHY AND EXHIBITIONS
INDEX OF NAMES
LIST OF COLORPLATES
CONTENTS

TEXT REFERENCES

[1] Georges Salles, Preface to the catalogue of the Rouault Exhibition, Musée d'Art Moderne, Paris, 1952.

[2] Neuchâtel (Switzerland), 1944. Preface by Claude Roulet.

[3] *Soliloques*, Neuchâtel, 1944, page 89.

[4] *Soliloques*, page 91.

[5] *La Renaissance*, Paris, October-December 1937.

[6] *Soliloques*, page 105.

[7] *Le Cirque de l'Etoile Filante*, Paris, 1938, page 65.

[8] *Soliloques*, page 104.

[9] *Soliloques*, Preface, pages 22 and 24.

[10] *Souvenirs Intimes*, Paris, 1926, page 82.

[11] *Le Cirque de l'Etoile Filante*, page 105.

[12] *Le Cirque de l'Etoile Filante*, page 10.

[13] Baudelaire, *Variétés critiques*, Paris, 1924, pages 104 and 105.

[14] Jacques Maritain, *Art et Scolastique*, Paris 1927.

[15] Baudelaire, *Variétés critiques*, Paris, 1924, pages 142 and 143.

[16] *La Revue Encyclopédique*, Paris, 1895, page 187.

[17] *La Revue Encyclopédique*, Paris, 1896, page 299.

[18] *Soliloques*, Preface, page 22.

BIBLIOGRAPHY

Monographs

M. Puy, *Georges Rouault*, Gallimard, Paris 1921. — G. Charensol, *Georges Rouault*, Les Quatre Chemins, Paris 1926. — R. Cogniat, *Georges Rouault*, Crès, Paris 1930. — R. Ito, *Rouault*, Atelier Sha, Tokyo 1936. — L. Venturi, *Georges Rouault*, E. Weyhe, New York 1940; 2nd edition, Skira, Paris 1948 (with an exhaustive bibliography). — E. A. Jewell, *Georges Rouault*, Hyperion, New York 1945. — J. T. Soby, *Georges Rouault, Painting and Prints*, Museum of Modern Art, New York 1945. — M. Brion, *Georges Rouault*, Braun, Paris 1950. — J. Lassaigne, *Rouault*, Skira, Geneva 1951. — J. Maritain, *Georges Rouault*, Abrams, New York 1952. — B. Dorival, *Cinq études sur Georges Rouault*, Editions universitaires, Paris 1956. — Shigetaro Fukushima, *Georges Rouault*, Skinchosha, Tokyo 1958. — P. Courthion, *Georges Rouault*, Abrams, New York 1962. — G. Marchiori, *Rouault*, Reynal, New York 1967.

Reminiscences

L. Bloy, *Quatre ans de captivité à Cochons sur Marne*, 1902-1904; *L'Invendable*, 1904-1907; *Le vieux de la montagne*, 1907-1910; *Au seuil de l'Apocalypse*, 1913-1915; *La porte des humbles*, 1915-1917; Mercure de France, Paris; *Notes sur Rouault*, Cahiers d'Art N° 3, 1928. — A. Suarès, *Lettres à Georges Rouault*, L'Art et les Artistes, April 1926. — A. Vollard, *Souvenirs d'un marchand de tableaux*, Albin Michel, Paris 1937. — Raïssa Maritain, *Les grandes amitiés*, 2 vols., Editions de la Maison française, New York 1941 and 1944. — *Correspondance entre A. Suarès et G. Rouault*, Gallimard, Paris 1960. — C. Roulet, *Rouault. Souvenirs*, Paris 1961.

Articles and Essays

Roger Marx, La Revue Encyclopédique, 1895 and 1896. — Gustave Geffroy, La Vie artistique, vol. V, 1897; vol. VI, 1900; vol. VII, 1901; vol. VIII, 1903. — C. Morice, Mercure de France, December 1905. — M. Puy, *Le dernier état de la peinture*, Le Feu, Paris 1910 (reprinted in *L'Effort des peintres modernes*, Paris 1933). — J. Rivière, Nouvelle Revue Française, 1910 (reprinted in Etudes N.R.F., Gallimard, Paris 1924). — R. Allard, La Revue Indépendante, January 1912. — G. Kahn, Mercure de France, January 1912. — L. Vauxcelles, Carnet des Artistes, 1917. — A. Salmon, Europe Nouvelle, November 28, 1920; L'Art Vivant, Paris 1920. — A. Warnod, L'Amour de l'Art, November 1920. — G. Coquiot, *Les Indépendants*, Paris 1920. — A. Lhote, L'Amour de l'Art, December 1923 (reprinted in *Parlons peinture*, Paris 1936). — G. Coquiot, *Des peintres maudits*, Delpeuch, Paris 1924. — J. Maritain, La Revue Universelle, 1924 (reprinted in *Art et Scolastique*, Paris 1927). — R. Fry, *La peinture moderne en France*, L'Amour de l'Art, May 1924. — W. George, Bulletin de la Vie artistique, May 15, 1924. — C. Einstein, Der Querschnitt, Berlin, March 1925. — A. Salmon, *Le Miserere de Georges Rouault*, L'Amour de l'Art, May 1925. — P. Courthion, *Panorama de la Peinture française contemporaine*, S. Kra, Paris 1927. — G. Chabot, Cahiers d'Art Nº 3, 1928; La Revue d'Art de Belgique, 1928. — C. Terrasse, Art d'aujourd'hui, 1928. — G. Charensol, L'Art Vivant, March 1929. — A. Malraux, Formes, December 1929. — R. H. Wilenski, Apollo I, London 1930. — L. L. Martin, Art et Décoration, April 1930. — C. Roger-Marx, *L'œuvre gravé de Georges Rouault*, Byblis, 1931. — M. Arland, Formes, 1931; Nouvelle Revue Française, July 1, 1931. — C. Zervos, Cahiers d'Art Nº 1-2, 1932. — M. Zahar, Formes, 1933. — W. Pach, Parnassus, New York, January 1933. — P. Fierens, L'Amour de l'Art, June 1933. — Sam A. Lewisohn, Parnassus, November 1933. — A. Lhote, Nouvelle Revue Française, August 1934. — Sheldon Cheney, *Expressionism in Art*, Liveright, New York 1934. — M. Dormoy, Arts et Métiers graphiques, August 1935. — W. Grohmann, in Thieme-Becker, *Allgemeines Lexikon der bildenden Künstler*, XXIX, Seemann, Leipzig 1935. — A. Blunt, Spectator, October 18, 1935. — C. Roulet, Belles-Lettres, Neuchâtel, December 1936 and May 1937. — M. de Vlaminck, *Désobéir*, Corréa, Paris 1936. — W. George, M. Dormoy, La Renaissance, special number, October-December 1937. — L. Gillet, Revue des Deux Mondes, July 1937. — M. Arland, Nouvelle Revue Française, August 1937. — R. Cogniat, Le Point, Lanzac, October 1937. — M. A. Couturier, Art Sacré, September 1938. — C. Zervos, *Histoire de l'art contemporain*, Cahiers d'Art, Paris 1938. — J. J. Sweeney, Parnassus, November 1938 and November 1939. — M. Davidson, Art News, New York, October 8, 1938; February 11, 1939. — T. McGreevy, The Studio, London, June 1939. — A. Suarès, Nouvelle Revue Française, 1940. — A. M. Frankfurter, Art News, May 11, 1940. — R. Speaight, Dublin Review, January 1941. — C. Roulet, Curieux, Neuchâtel, October 9, 1942. — L. Lehmann, J. de Laprade, G. Besson, Le Point, Lanzac, special number, August-October 1943. — D. Theote, *Intimate Moments with Rouault: Three Wars*, Tricolor, May 1944. — Una E. Johnson, *Ambroise Vollard éditeur*, Wittenborn, New York 1944. — L. Venturi, *Giorgio Rouault*, Lettere ed Arti, Venice, August 1946. — Abbé Maurice Morel, *Physionomie de Rouault*, Les Etudes, May 1947. — R. J. Douaire, *G. Rouault, His Art*, Liturgical Arts, New York, May 1948. — M. Arland, Hommes et Monde, March 1949. — J. Lassaigne, *L'œuvre gravé de Rouault*, Graphis, Zurich 1949. — B. Dorival, Les Musées de France, November 1950. — C. Zervos, *Approches de l'œuvre de Rouault*, Cahiers d'Art II, December 1952. — J. Pichard, Art d'église, Revue des Bénédictins de Saint-André, Bruges 1953. — F. Finne, Kunsten idag, 2, Oslo 1954. — J. Grenier, *Idées de G. Rouault*, L'Oeil, Paris, April 1957. — Special number of Mizue, *Homage to G. Rouault*, Tokyo 1958. — Abbé M. Morel, Les Etudes, April 1958. — S. Stehman, *La chapelle d'Hem*, Art d'église, Bruges 1958.

Illustrated Books

Souvenirs Intimes, text by Rouault, preface by A. Suarès, 6 original lithographs, Frapier, Paris 1926; 2nd edition with an original lithograph, 1927. — *Miserere*, 58 etchings and aquatints, pulled in 1927, published by Editions de l'Etoile Filante, Paris 1948. — *Petite Banlieue*, 6 lithographs, Cahiers des Quatre Chemins, Paris 1929. — *Paysages Légendaires*, poems by Rouault, with 6 lithographs and 50 drawings, Editions Porteret, Paris 1929. — *Les Carnets de Gilbert*, text by M. Arland, Nouvelle Revue Française, Paris 1931. — *Les Réincarnations du Père Ubu*, text by A. Vollard, 22 etchings and aquatints and 104 wood engravings, A. Vollard, Paris 1932. — *Le Cirque de l'Etoile Filante*, text by Rouault, 17 color etchings and 82 wood engravings, A. Vollard, Paris 1938. — *Passion*, text by A. Suarès, 17 color etchings and 82 wood engravings, A. Vollard, Paris 1938. — *Miserere*, reduced facsimile, Editions du Seuil, Paris 1951.

Soliloques, text by Rouault, preface by C. Roulet, 9 color plates, Ides et Calendes, Neuchâtel 1944. — *Divertissement*, text by Rouault, 15 color plates, Tériade, Paris 1943. — *Stella Vespertina*, text by Rouault, preface by Abbé Morel, 12 color plates, R. Drouin, Paris 1947.

Exhibitions

1895-1897, 1899-1901, Paris, Salon des Artistes Français. — 1902-1912, Paris, Salon des Indépendants. — 1903-1908, Paris, Salon d'Automne. — 1910, Paris, Galerie Druet (124 paintings, 54 ceramics). — 1911, Paris, Galerie Druet (45 paintings, 58 ceramics). — 1911, Paris, Salon d'Automne (18 paintings and ceramics). — 1920, November, Paris, Galerie La Licorne. — 1922, Paris, Galerie Barbazanges (pastels). — 1924, April-May, Paris, Galerie Druet (88 paintings). — 1925, Berlin and Düsseldorf, Galerie Flechtheim. — 1926, 1929, 1931, Paris, Galerie des Quatre Chemins. — 1927, Paris, Galerie Bing. — 1930, New York, Brummer Gallery. — 1930, London, St. George's Gallery. — 1930, Munich, Galerie Neumann (preface by Will Grohmann). — 1930, Chicago, Arts Club. — 1931, New York, Demotte Gallery. — 1931, Brussels, Galerie Schwarzenberg (preface by Paul Fierens). — 1931, Geneva, Galerie de l'Athénée. — 1933, New York, Pierre Matisse Gallery. — 1935, Northampton, Smith College Museum of Art. — 1935, London, Mayor Gallery. — 1936, Paris, Galerie Kaganovitch. — 1937, Paris, Musée du Petit-Palais, Rouault Room, "Masters of Independent Art." — 1937, New York, Pierre Matisse Gallery. — 1938, Basel, Kunsthalle (with Vlaminck and Raoul Dufy). — 1938, New York, Museum of Modern Art (prints, preface by M. Wheeler). — 1939, New York, Pierre Matisse Gallery. — 1940, New York, Bignou Gallery. — 1940-1941, Boston, Institute of Modern Art; Washington, Phillips Memorial Gallery; San Francisco, Museum of Art (introduction by L. Venturi). — 1941, New York, Marie Harriman Gallery. — 1942, Paris, Galerie Carré (10 paintings, preface by Bernard Dorival). — 1945,

New York, Museum of Modern Art (preface by James T. Soby and Carl O. Schniewind; 161 paintings, prints, sets and tapestries). — 1946, London, Tate Gallery (14 paintings and 25 prints from *Miserere*, preface by W. George). — 1946, Paris, Galerie Drouin, *Pour un art religieux* (17 paintings, 30 prints, preface by Abbé Morel). — 1946, Paris, Galerie Bing (with Modigliani, Soutine, Utrillo). — 1947, Prague, Gallery of the Circle of Intellectuals (10 paintings, 25 prints). — 1947, New York, Pierre Matisse Gallery. — 1947, Paris, Galerie des Garets. — 1948, Zurich, Kunsthaus (retrospective: 184 paintings, gouaches and watercolors; monotypes, lithographs and prints; preface by Abbé Morel). — 1948, Venice, Biennale (25 paintings). — 1948, Paris, Galerie des Garets (complete presentation of the *Miserere* prints). — 1949-1950, Traveling Exhibition of 26 paintings and prints from *Miserere* in Antwerp, La Louvière, Liège, Ghent, Rotterdam, Lille, Arras, Amiens, Besançon, Mulhouse (preface by Léon Lehmann), Karlsruhe, Munich, Freiburg-im-Breisgau (preface by Kurt Martin). The *Miserere* prints have since been exhibited in a great many cities and towns throughout France and Western Europe. — 1950, Buenos-Aires, Witcomb Gallery (*Miserere*, preface by Jorge Romero Brest). — 1950, Rome, Florence, Milan, exhibition of French religious art (*Miserere* prints, paintings and enamels, preface by Father Régamey). — 1950, Paris, Galerie Marigny (15 early works). — 1951, Stockholm, Samlaren Gallery, and Göteborg, Museum (16 paintings and some prints). — 1951, Paris, Musée d'Art Moderne, *Art Sacré* (22 paintings, preface by Jean Cassou), and Eindhoven Museum (Holland) (preface by Bernard Dorival). — 1951, Paris, Galerie de France (10 enamels executed at Ligugé). — 1952, Brussels, Palais des Beaux-Arts, and Amsterdam, Stedelijk Museum (78 paintings and prints, preface by Georges Salles and Lionello Venturi). — 1952, Paris, Musée d'Art Moderne (104 paintings, prints, ceramics, stained-glass windows, enamels, tapestries, preface by Georges Salles and Lionello Venturi). — 1953, Cleveland Museum of Art and New York, Museum of Modern Art (67 paintings and prints, preface by Jacques Maritain). — 1953, Los Angeles, County Museum (90 paintings, preface by Jacques Maritain). — 1953, Tokyo, National Museum, and Osaka (85 paintings and prints, preface by Marcel Arland). — 1954, Milan, Galleria d'Arte Moderna (114 paintings, prints, ceramics, stained-glass windows, enamels, tapestries; preface by Abbé Morel). — 1956, Paris, Galerie Creuzevault (enamels, prints). — 1956, Albi, Musée Toulouse-Lautrec (47 paintings, watercolors, gouaches, drawings, pastels, prints). — 1957, Rome, Galleria Odyssia (enamels). — 1958, Paris, Bibliothèque Nationale, *Hommage à Rouault*. — 1961, Ghent, Museum of Fine Arts, *Homage to Rouault*. — 1961, Los Angeles County Museum (prints). — 1964, Paris, Louvre, *Œuvres inachevées données à l'Etat*. — 1965, Paris, Galerie Charpentier, *Peintures inconnues ou célèbres*. — 1965, Geneva, Musée Rath, *La Passion*. — 1966, Frankfurt, Kunstverein. — 1969, Olten (Switzerland), Stadthaus, *Graphic Work from a Private Collection*.

INDEX OF NAMES

Rouault Georges (1871-1958), works:

Paintings:

1893 *Samson at the Mill* (Los Angeles) 5, 27;

1894 *The Child Jesus among the Doctors* (Colmar) 5, 8, 27, 35, 56, 113;

1895 *Christ mourned by the Holy Women* (Grenoble) 5, 27, 57;

1903 *Paris, Grey Weather* 42;
Portrait Study 42;
Prostitutes (watercolor, Bern) 31, 33, 42;
Tragic Clown (watercolor, Bern) 30;

1904 *Acrobat in Yellow*; *Circus Sketch*; *Circus Girl smoking*; *Clown*; *Clownesse*; *Fat Woman*; *Prostitute in a Red Dress*; *Pierrot and his Family* 42;
Head of a Tragic Clown (Montreux) 24, 31, 42;

1905 *Head of Christ* (New York) 44/46;
The Couple, M. et Mme Poulot (watercolor, Hem) 7, 45/47;

1906 *Party at the Waterside* (Paris) 43, 46;
Prostitute (watercolor and pastel, Paris) 31, 36, 54;
Prostitute before a Mirror (watercolor, Paris) 31, 37, 54;

1907 *"Aunt Sallys"* or *The Bride* (London) 50, 51;
Bathers (watercolor, Hem) 38, 56;
Circus Parade (watercolor and pastel, Montreux) 19, 46, 48;
Conjurer (Paris) 46, 49;
Odalisque (watercolor, Montreux) 31, 39, 54, 56;

1908 *Judges* (Copenhagen) 50;

1910 *Figures on the Steps, Park of Versailles* (watercolor, Paris) 3, 4;
Flood (Paris) 56, 57;
Pierrot (St. Louis) 51, 52, 54;
Prostitutes (Montreux) 55, 56;

1911 *Portrait of Mr. X* (Buffalo) 20, 22, 53, 54;

1913 *Three Judges* (New York) 61, 62; *Wrestlers* (New York) 62;

1917 *Old Clown* (Niarchos) 63, 65;

1918 *Crucifixion* (Philadelphia) 64, 65, 85, 96;

c. 1924 *Circus Trio* (Washington) 83, 85;

c. 1925 *The Prentice Craftsman* (Paris) 12, 85;

1927 *Grotesque* (Bern) 80, 85;

c. 1930 *Landscape beside the Sea* (New York) 86;

1930 *Cemetery* (pastel, Hem) 86;

after 1930 *Nude* (New York) 84, 85;

1930-1939 *Landscape* (Geneva) 86, 87;

c. 1933 *Little Family* (Paris) 9;
Wounded Clown (Paris) 9, 94, 96;

c. 1937 *Benito* 95;

1937 *The Dwarf* (Chicago) 91, 95;
The Last Romantic (New York) 88, 90;
The Old King (Pittsburgh) 89, 90, 95;

1937- *Head of Christ* (Cleveland)
1938 99, 101;
Polycarp (Solothurn) 93, 95;
Sunset (Worcester) 103, 106;
Twilight (Hem) 102;

1939 *Christ on the Lake of Tiberias* (Rome) 99, 106; *Crucifixion* (Paris) 96, 97;
Head of a Woman (Rome) 92, 95;

135

THE COLORPLATES

CONTENTS

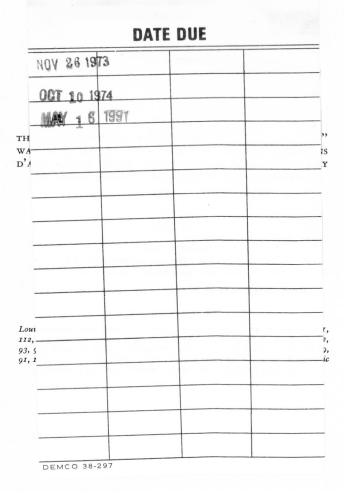

TH   ''

WA   IS

D'A   Y

Loui   *r,*

112,   *?,*

93, ç   *?,*

91, 1   *ic*

PRINTED IN SWITZERLAND